# Do You Require

## LEABHARLANNA CHONTAE FHINE GALL
## FINGAL COUNTY LIBRARIES

Items should be returned on or before the last date shown below. Items may be renewed by personal application, by writing or by telephone. To renew give the date due and the number on the barcode label. Fines are charged on overdue items and will include postage incurred in recovery. Damage to, or loss of items will be charged to the borrower.

| Date Due | Date Due | Date Due |
|----------|----------|----------|
| 30. JAN 03 | 19. NOV 05 | |
| 11. MAR 03 | | |
| 31. III 03 | | |
| 09. NOV 04 | Withdrawn from Stock | |
| 01 12. 04 | | |
| 25. FEB | | |
| 19. NOV | | |

UNITED KINGDOM
Sweet & Maxwell
London

AUSTRALIA
Law Book Co.
Sydney

CANADA and USA
Carswell
Toronto

HONG KONG
Sweet & Maxwell Asia

NEW ZEALAND
Brookers
Wellington

SINGAPORE and MALAYSIA
Sweet & Maxwell Asia
Singapore and Kuala Lumpur

What is the Law?

# Do You Require
# Planning Permission?

An Illustrated Guide (2nd Edition)

JOHN CREAN

B.A. HONS, MRUP, DIP. EIA MGMT, MRTPI, MIPI

DUBLIN
ROUND HALL PROFFESSIONAL PUBLISHING
2002

Published in 2002 by
Round Hall Sweet and Maxwell
43 Fitzwilliam Place
Dublin 2


Typeset and Printed by
Genprint, Dublin


ISBN 1-85800-299-0 9335


A catalogue record for this book
is available from the British Library

# Acknowledgments

Many thanks to Donal and Mona Crean for pretty much everything, Geraldine Crean, Geraldine O'Mahony, Keith Mitchell, Tom Phillips and Declan Brassil for their assistance and comments in the preparation of the first edition of this book and Ruth Mullins for her patience while this has been revised. Special thanks also to the staff of Round Hall for their assistance, without which this book would not have been published.

# About the Author

John Crean is a Town Planner with Cunnane Stratton Reynolds, Town Planners and Landscape Architects

# Table of Contents

# Introduction

## Exemptions from Planning Permission in General

The Planning system and many of the laws associated with it have recently been revised with the introduction of the Planning and Development Act 2000. This Act, which largely amalgamates and supersedes previous planning legislation enacted since 1963, also has implications for the types of development that are exempt from the requirement to obtain planning permission. This Act has also had an effect on the Planning Regulations, which also identify certain types of development that do not require planning permission.

This book will seek to identify some of the more commonplace exemptions that individuals and developers alike are entitled to avail of along with the limitations that one should be familiar with. It is a guide that is intended to provide an easy-to-use reference to the various exemptions from planning permission that are contained in the Local Government (Planning and Development) Regulations 2001 while also commenting on some of the relevant provisions of the Planning and Development Act 2000, explaining in simple terms the most likely interpretation of the exemptions from planning permission, and the conditions that must be met in order to obtain any benefit from them.

Hardstands for cars may only accommodate a maximum of two and must be located to the side or front of a house.

Following the old adage of "a picture tells a thousand words", the exemptions will be explained and clarified through a series of drawings and simple illustrations. Where illustrations do not assist in clarifying the provisions of any specific planning exemption, flow charts or notes are used. In all other cases, the language and requirements of the exemptions are simplified.

Where relevant, clarification of exemptions that lead to disagreements between Planners and Developers shall be offered. As "grey areas" do exist, it is always advisable that you should carefully consider whether or not the works or development you propose are exempted development as this often depends on the exact location of the development and the surrounding area; the various statutory restrictions that apply; and the planning history of the area, site, development and/or building.

In a different procedure to that which existed under previous planning legislation it is now possible to make a formal request to a Planning Authority for a "declaration" under section 5 of the 2000 Act for their view on whether or not a proposed development is in their opinion exempt from the need to obtain planning permission. If one does not agree with the view of the Planning Authority one can refer the decision to An Bord Pleanála for their definitive view. The section 5 procedure is outlined in Appendix 1.

As stated above, the 2000 Act is relevant to the question of what is or is not exempt from the requirement to obtain planning permission. Section 4 of the Act identifies developments considered exempt from planning permission. These are very broad definitions, not addressed in detail here, and one should only attempt to avail of any benefit from them after consultation with either the Planning Authority responsible for the area in which you plan to develop or with a Planning Consultant. Broad exemptions are identified in section 4(1) of the 2000 Act and are as follows:

(a) development consisting of the use of any land for the purpose of agriculture and development consisting of the use for that purpose of any building occupied together with land so used;

(b) development by the council of a county in its functional area, exclusive of any borough or urban district;

(c) development by the corporation of a county or other borough in that borough;

(d) development by the council of an urban district in that district;

(e) development consisting of the carrying out by the corporation of a county or other borough, or the council of a county or an urban district, of any works required for the construction of a new road or the maintenance or improvement of a road;

(f) development carried out on behalf of, or jointly or in partnership with, a local authority that is a planning authority, pursuant to a contract entered into by the local authority concerned, whether in its capacity as a planning authority or in any other capacity;

(g) development consisting of the carrying out by any local authority or statutory undertaker of any works for the purpose of inspecting, repairing, renewing, altering or removing any sewers, mains, pipes, cables, overhead wires, or other apparatus, including the excavation of any street or other land for that purpose;

(h) development consisting of the carrying out of works for the maintenance, improvement or other alteration of any structure, being works which affect only the interior of the structure or which do not materially affect the external appearance of the structure so as to render the appearance inconsistent with the character of the structure or of neighbouring structures;

(i) development consisting of the thinning, felling and replanting of trees, forests and woodlands, the construction, maintenance and improvement of non-public roads serving forests and woodlands and works ancillary to that development, not including the replacement of broadleaf high forest by conifer species;

(j) development consisting of the use of any structure or other land within the curtilage of a house for any purpose incidental to the enjoyment of the house as such;

(k) development consisting of the use of land for the purposes of a casual trading area (within the meaning of the Casual Trading Act 1995);

(l)   development consisting of the carrying out of any of the works referred to in the Land Reclamation Act 1949, not being works comprised in the fencing or enclosure of land which has been open to or used by the public within the ten years preceding the date on which the works are commenced.

The most common exemption that would apply to an urban context is (h) (above). Section 4(1)(h) can be used to exempt from planning permission all those external and internal works that occur to houses and other buildings that cannot be seen from outside the property. However, when the works affect the outside of the building, extreme care should be taken if one tries to obtain any benefit under this exemption.

A common domestic situation, however, where section 4(1)(h) may be applied is where "velux roof lights" are proposed. Under certain circumstances, but not under all circumstances, these may be exempt from requiring planning permission under section 4(1)(h). The above is an example of the fact that the application of the above exemptions is particularly subjective and one should always seek the advice of the Planning Authority prior to attempting to avail of any benefit under their provisions.

There are, however, limitations on exemptions that mean that all of the above may not apply in certain instances. These limitations on exemptions are contained in the Planning Regulations and are set out in Appendix 2.

## Warning

This document is only intended as a general guide and clarification of the provisions of the Local Government (Planning and Development) Regulations 2001. Any interpretations based on its contents should be carefully considered as the scenarios presented are very straightforward in planning terms. However, the issues do become very complex in "real life" and, as a result, the information and diagrams contained herein do not constitute professional advice for any particular proposal and should not be used as a substitute for professional advice. It should be noted by any individual seeking an exemption from planning permission that the development is often in such a location, or of such a design, or is subject to a Development Plan provision, or has a planning history which renders the application of the exemption provisions either uncertain or invalid.

It is important to recognise the following:

- Should any proposed development not fulfil the exact requirements for an exemption from planning permission, it will require planning permission.
- All illustrations contained in this book are indicative only. Where they are provided, they are intended to illustrate the exemptions from planning permission as they stand by the middle of 2002. They do not preclude other designs or layouts from complying with the requirements for an exemption from planning permission. They should not be used for design purposes.
- The interpretation of the exemptions from planning permission (as contained in the Local Government (Planning and Development) Regulations 2001 and

the Planning and Development Act 2000) and the decision as to whether a development is exempt from planning permission, is a matter for the Planning Authority or, ultimately, An Bord Pleanála.

● The fact that a development does not require planning permission does not remove any obligation or requirement under any other legislation that may apply. For example, the provisions of the Building Regulations/Building Control Act still apply even if a development is exempt from planning permission.

Having regard to the above, always check the following:

● Read the text of the exemptions in conjunction with this document and, if in doubt, seek the advice of planning consultants or professional planners in the Planning Authority as to whether or not the development does or does not require planning permission.

● Check any planning permission/development plan provision relating to the property to see if it invalidates any particular type of development which would ordinarily be exempt from the requirement to obtain planning permission, *e.g* a house extension may be invalid in certain instances. With development in a rural area, check with the County Council as to whether or not the proposed development is restricted by Special Areas of Conservation or any Proposed Natural Heritage Area.

● The various exemptions from planning permission are constantly subject to court cases and rulings that identify new interpretations of their particular meaning in certain circumstances. One should always be aware of this fact. This guide has, in attempting to clarify the provisions of the exemptions from planning permission contained in the Regulations, had regard, as far as possible, to the established position as of mid 2002.

# The Second Schedule

Local Government (Planning and Development) Regulations 2001
– Second Schedule

# Index of Exemptions from Planning Permission

## Chapter One
### Part One
### General Development

# Chapter Two

## Part Two
### Advertisements and Advertising Structures

# Chapter Three
## Part Three
## Rural Developments

# Chapter One – General Exemptions

This chapter addresses Part One of the Exempted Development section of the Planning and Development Regulations 2001. Part One provides for a wide range of exemptions from planning permission. As these provide for residential developments, they are most frequently the subject of queries to planning departments.

This section provides an interpretation of the exemptions that addresses some of the more common queries and misinterpretations that occur due to the wording of the "Exemptions". Each "Class" of Exemption shall be addressed in the same order in which it occurs in the Planning Regulations.

## Part One

# 1.1 Residential Developments[1]

## 1.1.1 Class 1 – An Extension to a House

The construction of an extension or conservatory does not require planning permission WHEN it is TO THE REAR of a house, subject to the following conditions:

(a) **Terraced and Semi-Detached Houses** – If the house has not previously been extended, the floor area of the proposed extension cannot exceed 40 sq. m. This exemption also allows for extensions above ground-floor level. (If the house is semi-detached or terraced, the area of the above-ground extension cannot exceed 12 sq. m.) In practical terms, for a typical semi-detached house, one could therefore have a ground-floor extension of 28 sq. m and a second-floor extension of 12 sq. m without applying for planning permission – unless one of the limitations on the exemption is breached.

If the proposed extension is in addition to an existing extension, the overall area of all extensions must be less than 40 sq. m (the previous extensions that one must take into account must be built after October 1, 1964 – including ones for which planning permission has been obtained) and the above limitations on ground- and upper-floor areas still apply. Therefore, if you own a typical semi-detached house and you already have an extension of 10 sq. m to the rear of the house, then you could build another 30 sq. m without planning permission. This could be entirely located on ground-floor level or some 12 sq. m could be located above ground level.

(b) **Detached Houses** – As with terraced and semi-detached houses, if the house has not previously been extended, the floor area of the proposed extension cannot exceed 40 sq. m. This exemption also allows for extensions above ground-floor level. (If the house is semi-detached or terraced, the area of the above-ground extension cannot exceed 20 sq. m). In practical terms, for a typical semi-detached house, one could therefore have a ground-floor extension of 20 sq. m and a second-floor extension of 20 sq. m without applying for planning permission – unless one of the limitations on the exemption is breached.

If the proposed extension is in addition to an existing extension, the overall area of all extensions must be less than 40 sq. m (the previous extensions that one must take into account must be built after October 1, 1964 – including ones for which planning permission has been obtained) and the above limitations on ground- and upper-floor areas still apply. Therefore, if you own a typical semi-detached house and you already have an extension

---

[1] It is important to note that the exemptions from planning permission that apply to houses, e.g. house extensions, are only available to "houses". The Planning Act specifically defines a house as a "building or part of a building which is being or has been occupied as a dwelling or was provided for use as a dwelling but has not been occupied, and where appropriate, includes a building which was designed for use as 2 or more dwellings or a flat, an apartment or other dwelling within such a building". This wording can be taken to mean that new houses under construction cannot avail of any of the exemptions until they have been built in accordance with their planning permission.

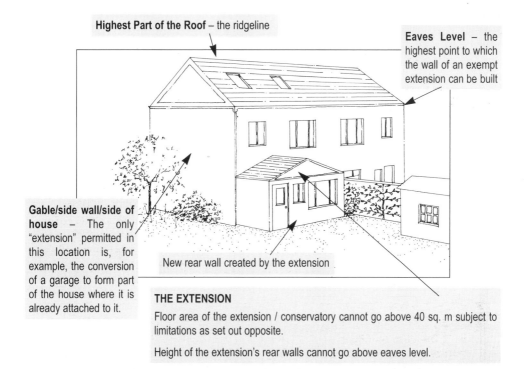

**Highest Part of the Roof** – the ridgeline

**Eaves Level** – the highest point to which the wall of an exempt extension can be built

**Gable/side wall/side of house** – The only "extension" permitted in this location is, for example, the conversion of a garage to form part of the house where it is already attached to it.

New rear wall created by the extension

**THE EXTENSION**

Floor area of the extension / conservatory cannot go above 40 sq. m subject to limitations as set out opposite.

Height of the extension's rear walls cannot go above eaves level.

The area of the rear garden (the private open space area used by the occupants of the house) must not go below 25 sq. m as a result of the extension. Open space to the side of the house should not be included in the calculation.

Planning Authorities often specify in their Development Plans or Local Area Plans what they consider to be "Private Open Space".

The shaded area on this drawing demonstrates the area that may be included in the 25 sq. m in calculating the 25 sq. m limit (assuming that the end of the rear wall is the end of the property).

of 10 sq.m to the rear of the house, then you could build another 30 sq. m without planning permission. This could be entirely located on ground-floor level or some 20 sq. m could be located above ground level.

(c)  The extension shall not reduce the "Private Open Space" of the back garden to less than 25 sq. m.

(d)  The ground floor extension shall not be closer than 2m from the boundary of the property.

(e)  The walls of the extension must not exceed the height of the rear wall of the building (or the side walls if the rear wall is a gable wall; see diagram following).

(f)  If the proposed extension has a flat roof, it must not exceed the eves or parapet level.

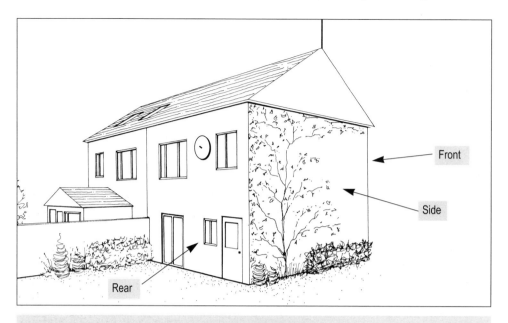

**Note: Building Lines – Determining where the rear of the house is**

A number of the exemptions from planning permission restrict development, allowing it under certain circumstances to occur either to the rear, front or side of a "house". In other instances, development to the front of a house is restricted so it does not occur beyond an established building line.

What is to the front, rear or side of a house is generally established by reference to notional building lines extending from the faces of any particular building. Establishing what area is the front, rear or side of a property is a particular problem where different building styles occur or where sites are not symmetrical. In such cases one should consult the Planning Authority for their views on an informal basis prior to proceeding with making a section 5 referral or making a planning application.

If an extension breaks an established building line, an exemption can be restricted (although this provision does not apply to Class 7, which deals with porches in front of a house).

(g)  If the proposed extension has a pitched roof, it must not exceed the ridge of the existing pitched roof.

(h)  Any window in the proposed extension at ground-floor level must not be less than 1m from the boundary it faces.

(i)  Any window in the proposed extension **above** ground-floor level must not be less than 11m from the boundary it faces. (For many typical semi-detached housing estates this limits all above-ground extensions as many of these houses already only have 11m from the rear wall of the house to the rear boundary).

(j)  Where the house is **detached** and the first floor extension exceeds 12 sq. m, any window in the proposed extension **above** ground-floor level must not be less than 11m from the boundary it faces.

(k)  The roof of any extension must not be used as a balcony or roof garden.

An extension TO THE SIDE of a house IS NOT EXEMPT under Class 1 and will require planning permission. The only "extension", to the side of a house, that does not require planning permission is one that involves the CONVERSION for use AS PART OF

THE HOUSE of:

- a garage;
- a shed;
- a store; or
- other similar structure.

These must be attached to the house prior to conversion.

**Note:**

(a) The "gable" of a roof is most likely to be interpreted as triangular in shape.

(b) Also refer to Class 3, as this has potential implications for the size of extensions that may be built in certain circumstances.

(c) This exemption does not apply where a Special Amenity Area Order is in effect (see Appendix 2).

(d) It is important to note that the exemptions from planning permission that apply to houses, *e.g.* house extensions, are only available to "houses". The Planning Act specifically defines a house as a "building or part of a building which is being or has been occupied as a dwelling or was provided for use as a dwelling but has not been occupied, and where appropriate, includes a building which was designed for use as 2 or more dwellings or a flat, an apartment or other dwelling within such a building". This wording can be taken to mean that new houses under construction cannot avail of any of the exemptions until they have been built in accordance with their planning permission.

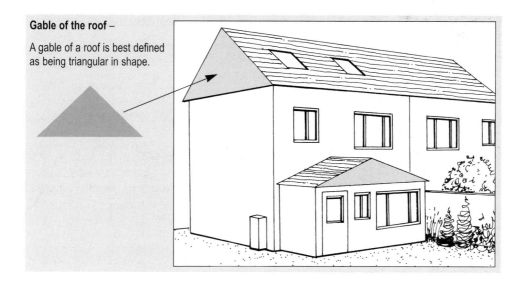

**Gable of the roof –**

A gable of a roof is best defined as being triangular in shape.

### 1.1.2    Class 2 – Providing a "Structure" as Part of a House's Central Heating System – a Chimney, Boiler House or Oil Tank

This exemption is relatively straightforward in what it allows. It permits the provision of:

- an oil tank;
- a chimney;
- a boiler house

as part of a house's Central Heating System only. The exemption is subject to the following conditions:

- The oil tank, chimney or boiler house must be provided as part of a "house" (a house that is lived in).
- Any proposed oil tank shall not exceed a capacity of 3,500 litres – this is the only restriction on the size of any of the above.

The finish of any chimney or boiler house may be restricted by the limitations attached to exemptions under Class 3. Class 3 deals with the "construction/placing of sheds and similar structures in the grounds of a house" (see below).

**Note:**

The conditions restricting exemptions under Class 3 state that certain similar structures (this includes garages) located TO THE SIDE of a house must have the same wall and roof finish as the house itself. This may be interpreted as applying to a boiler house. Therefore, if the side-wall finish of the house is rendered plaster, the boiler house (if located and attached to the side of the house) may also have to be rendered plaster.

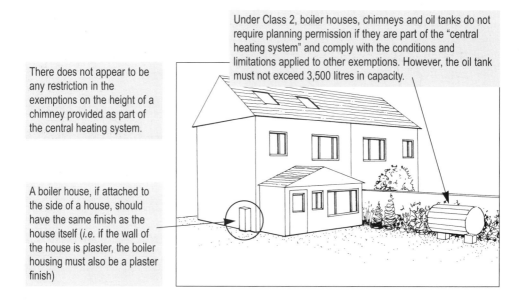

There does not appear to be any restriction in the exemptions on the height of a chimney provided as part of the central heating system.

A boiler house, if attached to the side of a house, should have the same finish as the house itself (*i.e.* if the wall of the house is plaster, the boiler housing must also be a plaster finish)

Under Class 2, boiler houses, chimneys and oil tanks do not require planning permission if they are part of the "central heating system" and comply with the conditions and limitations applied to other exemptions. However, the oil tank must not exceed 3,500 litres in capacity.

### 1.1.3    Class 3 – Construction or Placing Sheds and Similar Structures in the Grounds of a House

This is a relatively broad exemption that allows a number of different types of structures to be constructed, placed or erected within the grounds of a house without planning permission. Class 3 means that planning permission is not necessary under certain conditions for any:

- shed or similar structure;
- tent;
- awning;
- shade or other object;
- greenhouse;
- garage; or
- store.

In order to be exempt from planning permission the above structures must satisfy all of the following:

- They must not be located in front of the house, *i.e.* beyond the "line" of the front wall of the house.
- The total area of the structures proposed, when taken together with other such structures (as listed above) anywhere on the site ("within the curtilage of the dwelling"), regardless of when they were built, MUST NOT EXCEED 25 sq. m  in area.
- The "Private Open Space" in the garden TO THE REAR OR SIDE of the house must never drop below 25 sq. m.
- Any structure (this includes garages) located TO THE SIDE of a house must have the same, or similar, wall and roof finish as the house.
- If the structure has a flat roof, it must not exceed 3m in height. Pitched roof, tiled or slated structures must not exceed 4m in height.
- The structure provided CANNOT be used for housing humans, pigs, poultry, horses, ponies or pigeons.
- The structure must be used for a purpose associated with the use of the house as a dwelling.

**Note:**
  (a)  This Class of exemption should also be considered in light of the provisions of Classes 1 and 2.
  (b)  This exemption does not apply where a Special Amenity Area Order is in effect (see Appendix 2).

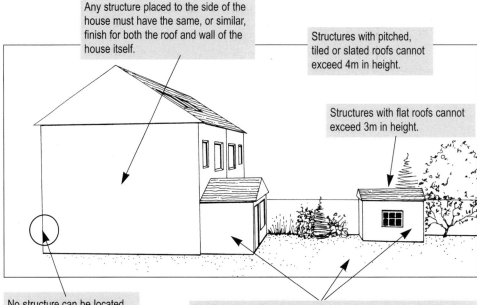

Any structure placed to the side of the house must have the same, or similar, finish for both the roof and wall of the house itself.

Structures with pitched, tiled or slated roofs cannot exceed 4m in height.

Structures with flat roofs cannot exceed 3m in height.

No structure can be located forward of the front wall of the house under this exemption.

The floor area of any structure, *i.e.* a shed, either on its own or together with any existing extensions or structures, must not reduce the area of the rear garden to less than 25 sq. m.

No such structure can be used as a living space for people, or to house pigs, poultry, pigeons, ponies or horses. It can, however, be used for a purpose incidental to the enjoyment of the house.

**Note:**
The construction of a house extension (under Class 1) and the provision of a shed (under Class 3) may be a difficulty in many modern house sites as it may reduce the area of private open space to less than 25 sq. m and consequently require planning permission.

### 1.1.4 Class 4 – Wireless, TV Antennae and Satellite Dishes – When Do They Need Planning Permission?

Class 4 exempts the erection of TV, Radio Antennae and Satellite Dishes from planning permission. These exemptions are QUALIFIED BY considerations of LOCATION and SIZE.

#### TV and Wireless Antennae

The erection of TV or wireless antenna on the roof of a dwelling does not require planning permission ONLY where it does not exceed the height of the dwelling by 6m (*i.e.* 6m above the ridge height of the roof).

It is important to note that this exemption only applies to the erection of a wireless or TV antennae "on the roof of a house". The location of the antennae on any other part of the dwelling, or within its site boundary, is not catered for by this condition.

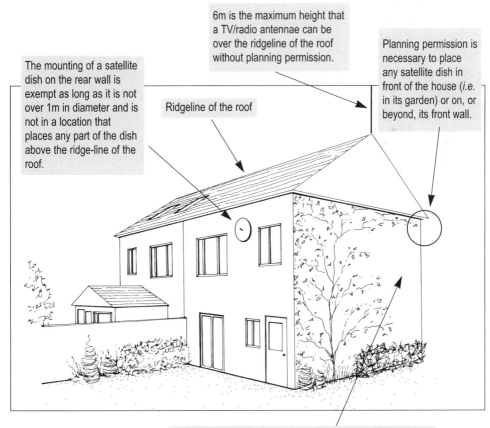

6m is the maximum height that a TV/radio antennae can be over the ridgeline of the roof without planning permission.

Planning permission is necessary to place any satellite dish in front of the house (*i.e.* in its garden) or on, or beyond, its front wall.

The mounting of a satellite dish on the rear wall is exempt as long as it is not over 1m in diameter and is not in a location that places any part of the dish above the ridge-line of the roof.

Ridgeline of the roof

A satellite dish may be placed on a gable/side wall but must neither protrude beyond the front wall nor above the ridgeline of the roof.

**Note:**

This exemption may be limited if the building on which it is to be placed is listed for preservation in the Development Plan or the Draft Development Plan for the area in which the development is proposed. As a result, you may wish to discuss with the Planning Authority the relevance of section 4(1)(h) exemptions in such cases.

### Satellite Dishes

ONLY ONE Satellite Dish on a dwelling, or within its site, can be exempt from planning permission. This dish MUST NOT:

- be mounted either on, or in front of, the front wall of the house (*e.g.* not placed in the front garden);
- be more than 1m in diameter; or
- be located on the front slope of the roof, or higher than the roof's ridgeline.

**Note:**

(a) Only one satellite dish is specified as being exempt. If you want to locate additional satellite dishes on a property, you must apply for planning permission irrespective of where they are located if there is already one "exempted" dish on the property. The proposed dish can transmit as well as receive signals.

(b) Many satellite TV suppliers erect dishes in locations where permission is required. Planning authorities may take enforcement action in such cases.

## 1.1.5 Class 5 – The Construction of Walls, Gates, Fences and Railings around Houses

Class 5 allows certain structures, such as walls, to be built without planning permission (under certain conditions) around a house or within its boundary. The list of items open for possible exemption includes:

- a gate;
- a gateway;
- a railing;
- a wooden fence; or
- walls built in either brick, stone, blocks (including concrete blocks) or mass concrete.

The main requirement of Class 5 is that the construction, erection or alteration of any of the above WILL NOT REQUIRE planning permission IF:

- they are within or bounding the site of a dwelling;
- they do not exceed 1.2m in height when in front of the dwelling;
- they do not exceed 2m in height when behind the front wall of the dwelling.

The height of any wall or similar structure permitted under this exemption should not exceed 2m. Where this wall or such similar structure bounds an area in front of a house, it should not exceed 1.2m without planning permission.

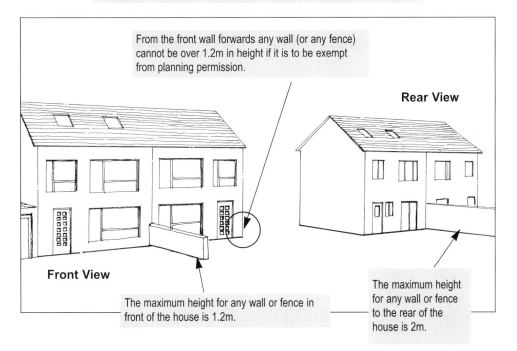

From the front wall forwards any wall (or any fence) cannot be over 1.2m in height if it is to be exempt from planning permission.

Rear View

Front View

The maximum height for any wall or fence in front of the house is 1.2m.

The maximum height for any wall or fence to the rear of the house is 2m.

Any wall, NOT INCLUDING FENCES, built to the above exempted heights must also be:

- capped (unless it is a dry stone wall); or
- plastered, unless it is made from decorative blocks/bricks, where it bounds a garden/or some other space between a dwelling-house and a road.

**Note:**

   (a) Where a proposed gate involves the formation, laying out or material widening of a means of access to a public road the surfaced carriageway of which exceeds 4m in width, planning permission is required.

   (b) If the structure does not meet all of the above requirements, then planning permission is required.

   (c) The basic "rule of thumb" is that anything in front of the house cannot be higher than 1.2m and anything behind the front wall of the house can be up to 2m in height (see diagram following and Class 1 diagrams).

   (d) Where gates or gateways are involved, this exemption does not apply where the work proposed involves the making, laying out or material widening of an access (*e.g.* a gateway) to a surfaced public road where the surfaced carriageway of that road exceeds 4m in width. Furthermore, the Planning Authority may consider this exemption not to apply if they believe that a traffic hazard or obstruction to road users may be created. It is therefore advisable that you check any such proposal with the Planning Authority prior to commencing works (see Appendix 2).

   (e) This provision does not apply to any metal or palisade fencing.

## 1.1.6    Class 6 – The Construction of Paths, Drains, Ponds, Landscaping Works or a Hardstand within the Boundary of a House

Class 6 deals with the construction of any:

- path;
- drain;
- pond;
- landscaping; or
- hardstands, *i.e.* areas for parking cars.

### Paths, Drains, Ponds and Landscaping

Many different types may be constructed and will be exempt from planning permission as long as:

- the level of the ground shall not be altered by more than 1m above or below the level of the adjoining ground.

### Note:

The Planning Authority may disagree with any individuals carrying out landscape works where they are considered to be excessive – for example, if large amounts of soil are moved or if gardens are raised to create a situation where they overlook an adjoining neighbour's property.

### Hardstands/Hard Surface Areas

The following do not require planning permission:

- The provision of a hard area, *i.e.* a patio to the REAR of a dwelling for any purpose INCIDENTAL to the enjoyment of that dwelling.
- The provision of a hardstand/hard surface area for up to TWO CARS to the FRONT or SIDE of a dwelling for any purpose INCIDENTAL to the enjoyment of that dwelling.

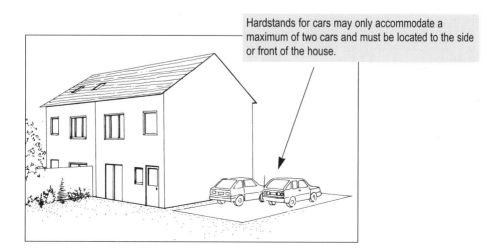

Hardstands for cars may only accommodate a maximum of two cars and must be located to the side or front of the house.

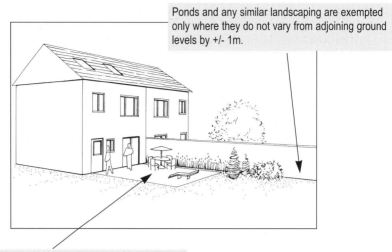

Ponds and any similar landscaping are exempted only where they do not vary from adjoining ground levels by +/- 1m.

Hard surface areas to the rear of the house are exempted development provided they are used for a purpose incidental to the enjoyment of the house. They are not to be used for the parking of cars.

**Note:**
Class 13 limits private paved areas and footpaths to no more then 3m in width. This may be relevant to this exemption in certain cases.

**Note:**

- It could be argued that the stipulation that the works do not vary 1m +/- the adjoining ground levels also applies to the provision of a hardstand. Therefore, the potential exists for either a raised or sunken hardstand, although this may be challenged by the Planning Authority or a neighbour.

## 1.1.7 Class 7 – Constructing a Porch outside any House

The construction of a porch outside any EXTERNAL door to a house, generally considered to be the FRONT DOOR, does not require planning permission if:

- the front wall of the extension/porch is not less than 2m from any road;
- it has a floor area of not more than 2 sq. m;
- it is less than 4m in height if it has a pitched roof (tiled or slated);
- it is less than 3m in height in any other instance (*e.g.* if it has a flat roof).

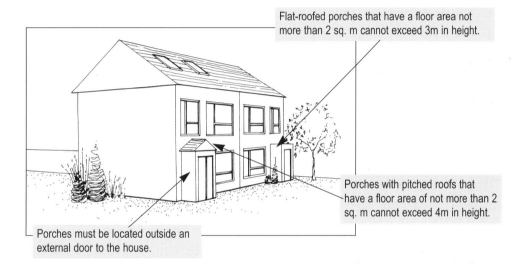

Flat-roofed porches that have a floor area not more than 2 sq. m cannot exceed 3m in height.

Porches with pitched roofs that have a floor area of not more than 2 sq. m cannot exceed 4m in height.

Porches must be located outside an external door to the house.

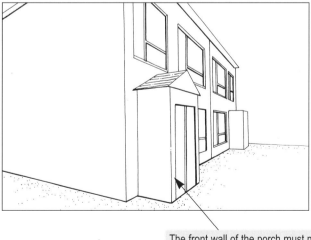

The front wall of the porch must not be less than 2m from the road.

### 1.1.8    Class 8 – Storing a Boat, Caravan or Campervan within the Grounds of a House

Class 8 allows for the storage of either ONE campervan, caravan OR boat within the grounds of a house.

The storage is only exempt from planning permission where the following conditions are satisfied:

- The house should be lived in.
- The boat, caravan or campervan cannot be lived in while stored.
- It must not be kept stored for more than nine months in any year.
- It cannot be used for either storing, selling or advertising any goods (*e.g.* any business purpose).
- It shall not be used for any business while stored.

**Note:**

The result of this exemption is that a caravan or boat can only be stored on the grounds of a house for nine months of any year and absolutely nothing must be done with it.

## 1.1.9 Class 9 – Constructing a Gate or Gateway

Class 9 exempts the construction, erection, replacement or renewal of:

- any gate; or
- gateway

from planning permission.

The exemption is subject to the following conditions:

- The gate or gateway CANNOT be located in the grounds of a house, NOR can it form part of a boundary to a house.
- It CANNOT be higher than 2m.

**Note:**

This exemption does not apply where the work proposed involves the making, laying out or material widening of an access (*e.g.* a gateway) to a surfaced public road where the surfaced carriageway of that road exceeds 4m in width. Furthermore, the Planning Authority may consider this exemption not to apply if they believe that a traffic hazard or obstruction to road users may be created. It is therefore advisable that you check any such proposal with the Planning Authority prior to commencing works (see Appendix 2).

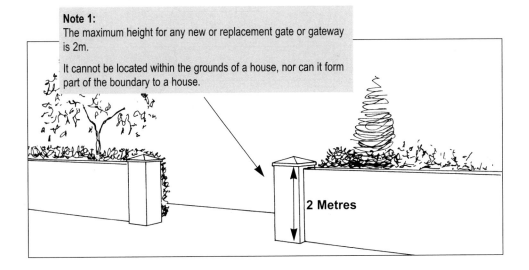

**Note 1:**
The maximum height for any new or replacement gate or gateway is 2m.

It cannot be located within the grounds of a house, nor can it form part of the boundary to a house.

2 Metres

**Note 2:**
See Class 5 for the construction of a gate or gateway within the grounds of a house, or as part of the boundary to a house.

### 1.1.10   Class 10 – Plastering or Capping any Concrete Wall or a Wall Made from Concrete Blocks

Plastering or capping any concrete wall does not require planning permission.

However, should the wall be capped, it is important to note that the cap stones will become part of the wall and therefore will be subject to the restrictions on height specified in Class 5. Therefore, any wall, capping included, MUST NOT exceed 2m if located to the rear of the house, or 1.2m if located to the front of the house, to benefit from this exemption. (See Class 5 for more information on walls in a residential area).

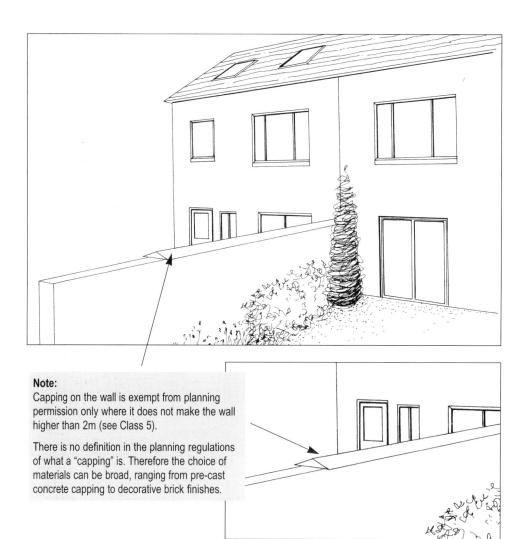

**Note:**
Capping on the wall is exempt from planning permission only where it does not make the wall higher than 2m (see Class 5).

There is no definition in the planning regulations of what a "capping" is. Therefore the choice of materials can be broad, ranging from pre-cast concrete capping to decorative brick finishes.

## 1.1.11   Class 11 – The Construction, Erection, Lowering, Repair or Replacement of Fences and Walls

This class deals with the construction of any wall that is not located around a house or within its boundaries.

Class 11 applies to:

- fences (NOT INCLUDING sheet metal fences or hoardings); and
- any wall of stone, brick, blocks with a decorative finish, concrete blocks or mass concrete.

The exemption is restricted as follows:

- The height of any new structure/wall/fence CANNOT exceed 1.2m OR the height of the wall or fence being replaced, whichever is the greater, *i.e.* if the wall being replaced is only 1.5m in height, then the replacement wall can be built no higher than this. If the existing wall is only 1m in height then its replacement can be built up to 1.2m. However, any new or replacement wall or structure cannot exceed 2.0m in height in any event; if it does, planning permission is required.
- Every wall erected with the benefit of this exemption next to a road must be capped and plastered. (This does not apply if the wall is a dry stone wall or one made using decorative bricks.)

The exemption and the conditions that apply are similar to those of Class 5, which deals with walls in and around the boundary of the house.

**Note:**

- (a) This exemption does not apply where a Special Amenity Area Order is in effect (see Appendix 2).
- (b) While fences come within the scope of this exemption, SHEET METAL FENCES and HOARDINGS do not.

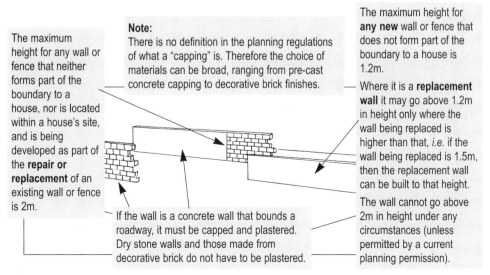

The maximum height for any wall or fence that neither forms part of the boundary to a house, nor is located within a house's site, and is being developed as part of the **repair or replacement** of an existing wall or fence is 2m.

**Note:**
There is no definition in the planning regulations of what a "capping" is. Therefore the choice of materials can be broad, ranging from pre-cast concrete capping to decorative brick finishes.

If the wall is a concrete wall that bounds a roadway, it must be capped and plastered. Dry stone walls and those made from decorative brick do not have to be plastered.

The maximum height for **any new** wall or fence that does not form part of the boundary to a house is 1.2m.

Where it is a **replacement wall** it may go above 1.2m in height only where the wall being replaced is higher than that, *i.e.* if the wall being replaced is 1.5m, then the replacement wall can be built to that height.

The wall cannot go above 2m in height under any circumstances (unless permitted by a current planning permission).

## 1.1.12   Class 12 – The Painting of any Part of a Building

Planning permission is not required for any alteration to a house or other structure that consists solely of:

- the painting of any external part of the building or structure.

This permits the painting of a house, building or structure. The only limitation is that painting cannot be carried out in order to create a mural.

The only occasion when the painting of a mural is exempted is when it is carried out on a HOARDING or "other temporary structure" bounding (*i.e.* surrounding) land where development is to be carried out. An example of this exemption includes the creation of murals on wooden hoardings that are located around building sites.

**Note:**

Buildings that are Protected Structures, or those in an Architectural Conservation Area in either Draft or adopted Development Plans may be affected by this provision. See Appendix 2 for restrictions.

**Note:**
Conditions can be attached to planning permissions requiring any particular structure to be of a certain colour, in which case this exemption would still apply but the choice of colour would be restricted.

The painting of the external surface of any structure is exempted development unless it conflicts with the conditions of a planning permission.

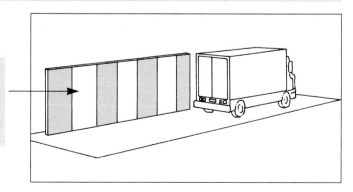

Murals require planning permission. However, structures, such as hoardings, may be painted with murals under certain conditions (see above).

## 1.1.13   Class 13 – Private Road Ways and Footpaths

The following is exempted development:

- REPAIRING or IMPROVING any PRIVATE ROAD, WAY or STREET – this exemption appears to exclude the possibility of extending or widening a private road or way, *i.e.* it may be repaired but not made wider.

- Provision of any PRIVATE FOOTPATH or PAVING (the width shall not exceed 3m).

While the illustration below shows a residential situation, this exemption applies to all private roads or ways, *i.e.* a private road leading from the public road to a factory, golf course or house located away from the road.

**Note:**
Class 6, which deals with development on lands within the boundary of a residential property, may also be relevant.

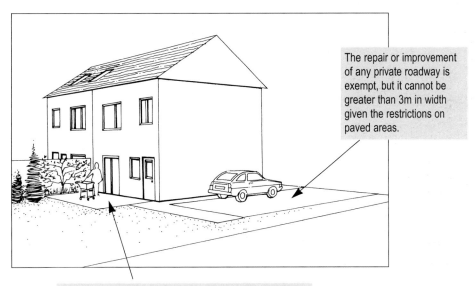

The repair or improvement of any private roadway is exempt, but it cannot be greater than 3m in width given the restrictions on paved areas.

Class 13 limits private paved areas and footpaths to no more than 3m in width.

# 1.2 Changes of Use

## 1.2.1 Class 14 – Changes of Use

CHANGING THE USE of a building or structure from one use to another generally requires planning permission. However, under certain circumstances it is exempt from planning permission.

Class 14 allows for three specific "types" of change of use. These principally involve changes of use to a:

- shop;
- house/dwelling; or
- residence for persons with special needs (persons with an intellectual or physical disability)

from other specified uses.

**Note:**

Part IV of the Second Schedule of the Local Government (Planning and Development) Regulations 2001 sets out various Classes of Use for properties. Classes 1 to 11 of Part IV are outlined on the following pages. **A change from one use to another requires planning permission, except where it involves a change from a Class 2 use to a Class 1 use**. However, a change within a Use Class does not require planning permission. Changes to the exterior of the structure as a result of the change of use may require planning permission and the relevant Planning Authority should be consulted on this point.

**Shop – For Use As...**

A property with a use listed below can be changed into a shop without planning permission (the reverse does not necessarily apply):

1. as a hot food take-away;
2. as a car sales/motor vehicles (or leasing) showroom;
3. as a public house;
4. as a restaurant;
5. as a funeral home (or somewhere that funerals are organised/directed);
6. as an amusement arcade;
7. for the provision of financial services, *i.e.* a bank;
8. for the provision professional services (not health or medical);
9. for the provision of "any other" services; or
10. as a betting office.

**Dwelling – For Use As...**

Where a building consists of two or more dwellings, it may be reconverted for use as a single dwelling without planning permission. However, the two (or more) dwellings must previously have been used as a single dwelling. For example, where a building previously used as flats or bedsits is reconverted into a family home.

### Residence – For Use As...

A house may be made into a residence for persons with an intellectual or physical disability without planning permission if:

1. the residence is to care for persons with an "intellectual or physical disability or a mental illness";
2. the number of residents with any such disability does not exceed SIX;
3. the number of carers, caring for the residents, does not exceed TWO.

### Note:

Be aware of the following when considering a "Change of Use".

### Material Works

Changes to the PHYSICAL APPEARANCE of any building that are necessary as part of a change of use, such as THE PROVISION OF A NEW SHOP FRONT, may require planning permission as the Local Authority may consider that the changes materially alter the appearance of the property.

### An Abandoned Use

If the use of a property is considered by the Planning Authority to be abandoned, a change of use ordinarily exempt may require planning permission. For example, the change of use of a car sales showroom to a shop is exempt. However, if the car sales showroom has not been in use for a number of years, then the use is said to have lapsed. Therefore planning permission is required. However, under Article 10(1)(d) of the Planning Regulations a change of use from an unauthorised use is not exempt unless it is to return to a permitted use (that has not been abandoned).

### Note:

Should a change of use be proposed in such circumstances, it should be checked with the planning authority beforehand.

### Changes within Use Classes

Under Part IV of the Second Schedule of the Local Government (Planning and Development) Regulations 2001 certain property uses, due to their nature and impact, are grouped into the same class of use. Any change within a use class (where the existing use is permitted) will be exempt (although previous planning permissions relating to the property should be checked). Any change between classes of use will not be exempt except for changes from Class 2 to Class 1.

These Use Classes are listed in the Local Government (Planning and Development) Regulations 2001 as follows:

### CLASS 1

Use as a shop.

**CLASS 2**

Use for the provision of the following services where these services are provided principally to visiting members of the public.:

   (a)  financial services;

   (b)  professional services (other than health or medical services);

   (c)  any other services (including use as a betting office).

**CLASS 3**

Use as an office, other than a use to which Class 2 applies.

**CLASS 4**

Use as a light industrial building.

**CLASS 5**

Use as a wholesale warehouse or as a repository.

**CLASS 6**

Use as a residential club, a guest house or a hostel (other than a hostel where care is provided).

**CLASS 7**

Use:

   (a)  for public worship or religious instruction;

   (b)  for the social or recreational activities of a religious body;

   (c)  as a monastery or convent.

**CLASS 8**

Use:

   (a)  as a health centre or clinic or for the provision of any medical or health services (but not the use of the dwelling-house of a consultant or practitioner, or any building attached to the dwelling-house or within the curtilage thereof, for that purpose);

   (b)  as a creche;

   (c)  as a day nursery;

   (d)  as a day centre.

**CLASS 9**

Use:

   (a)  for the provision of residential accommodation and care to people in need of care (but not the use of a dwelling-house for that purpose);

   (b)  as a hospital or nursing home;

   (c)  as a residential school, residential college or residential training centre.

**CLASS 10**

Use:

   (a)  as an art gallery (but not for the sale or hire of works of art);

   (b)  as a museum;

   (c)  as a public library or public reading room;

   (d)  as a public hall;

   (e)  as an exhibition hall;

   (f)  as a social centre, community centre or non-residential club; but not as a dance hall or concert hall.

**CLASS 11**

Use:

   (a)  as a theatre;

   (b)  as a cinema;

   (c)  as a concert hall;

   (d)  as a bingo hall;

   (e)  as a skating rink or gymnasium or for other indoor sports or recreation not involving the use of motorised vehicles or firearms.

## Excluded Uses

Under Article 10(2)(b) of the Local Government (Planning and Development) Regulations 2001, certain types of use are excluded from any exemptions that provide for a change of use within use classes outlined in Part IV of the Second Schedule of the Local Government (Planning and Development) Regulations 2001. These include the use of a property as:

 ● an amusement arcade;

 ● a motor service station/petrol station;

 ● a car sales or leasing garage/office;

 ● a taxi/hackney/vehicle hire premises;

 ● a scrapyard/car(vehicle) breaker's yard;

 ● a mineral storage and distribution location;

 ● a supermarket, the total net retail sales space of which exceeds 3,500 sq. m in the Greater Dublin Area and 3,000 sq. m in the remainder of the State;

 ● a retail warehouse, the total gross retail sales space of which exceeds 6,000 sq. m (including any ancillary garden centre);

 ● a shop, associated with a petrol station, the total net retail sales space of which exceeds 100 sq. m.

## Definitions

The Local Government (Planning and Development) Regulations 2001 provide important definitions that should always be examined when considering changes of use. It defines many uses in detail and is important in determining what is or is not exempt from planning permission.

These definitions are contained in Appendix 3 as they appear in the Planning Regulations.

## 1.2.2    Class 15 – Occasional Use of Buildings for Social and Recreational Use

Class 15 allows for the occasional use of a number of types of buildings for SOCIAL and RECREATIONAL PURPOSES. Buildings where occasional social and recreational activities will not require planning permission include:

- schools;
- halls;
- clubs;
- art galleries;
- museums;
- libraries;
- reading rooms;
- gymnasiums; and
- any "structure"/building used for public worship or "religious instruction" (*i.e.* churches).

A typical, although contentious, example of the use of this exemption would be an instance where a "school disco" is held at a school hall/gymnasium. It should be noted, however, that the use of any hall for a purpose such as a disco, on a repeated basis rather than occasionally, as specified in the Planning Regulations, might lead to enforcement proceedings by the Local Authority.

**Note:**

(a) Under Class 15 the "social and recreational" uses would be expected to have a limited impact. It is, therefore, important that the various associated impacts of each particular "occasional" use are considered carefully prior to maintaining that this exemption applies (see flow diagram).

(b) It should be noted that Class 15 and the interpretation of "occasional" is contextual and may be the subject of disagreement between the planning authority and the public/developers.

**Occasional... A Key Word**

When deciding whether a use can be described as "occasional" the following should be taken into account:

← 

(1) The number of times the proposed temporary use occurs.

(2) The scale and impact of the proposed temporary use.

(3) The location of the proposed temporary use.

(4) Has a precedent established the use of the building for "social or recreational" purposes?

(5) The character of the surrounding area.

# 1.3 Temporary Structures

## 1.3.1 Class 16 – Temporary Works and Structures

Class 16 allows for the temporary "erection, construction or placing" of plant or machinery structures on land.

To be exempt from planning permission, however, these TEMPORARY works or structures must be required for the construction of any development that is either exempted development, or has been granted planning permission.

Exempted development in this instance ONLY includes:

- the erection, placing or construction of any structures, works, plant or machinery.

These structures, plant or machinery must be:

- "needed temporarily" during the time period when the development is being carried out;
- required in connection with the terms or conditions of a planning permission or exempted development;
- located on, in or under the relevant lands or on adjoining land; and
- removed when the development is complete and the land returned to its original condition (unless an alteration has been permitted under a planning permission).

**Note:**

(a) The works that are exempted in this instance do not include mining.

(b) Legal interest must be held over the lands on which the temporary structures/works are to be located.

(c) A licence may be required from the relevant County Council, City Council or Town Council in order to construct such temporary structures either on public footpaths or roads.

(d) This exemption does not apply where a Special Amenity Area Order is in effect (see Appendix 2).

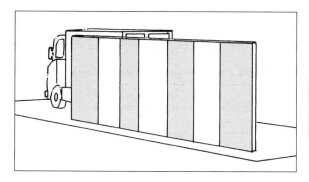

Hoardings outside building sites and associated construction machinery can avail of this exemption.

### 1.3.2    Class 17 – Temporary Accommodation for Works

Class 17 allows for the temporary "erection, construction or placing" of on-site accommodation for those involved in development for permitted development works.

To be exempt from planning permission, however, this TEMPORARY on-site accommodation must be required for the construction of any development that either is exempted development or has been granted planning permission.

This temporary on-site accommodation must be:

- "needed temporarily" during the time period when the development is being carried out;
- located on, in or under the relevant lands or on adjoining land; and
- removed when the development is complete and the land returned to its original condition (unless an alteration has been permitted under a planning permission).

**Note:**
 (a)   The works that are exempted in this instance do not include mining.
 (b)   Legal interest must be held over the lands on which the temporary structures/works are to be located.

### 1.3.3    Class 18 – Temporary Structures (Mining)

The TEMPORARY erection, placing or construction of any structures, works, plant or machinery on, in or under land where mining works are to be carried out does not require planning permission where:

- the temporary structures are needed in the PREPARATION of the land for mining;
- the mining is to take place on the land IN ACCORDANCE WITH a planning permission; and
- the temporary structures are removed before mining takes place (when the mine and any ancillary structures are commissioned).

**Note:**
The temporary structures can also be placed on adjoining land.

### 1.3.4 Class 19 – Temporary Facilities (Provision of Such on Behalf of State Authorities)

Either developing, providing, constructing or erecting:

- any temporary structures or facilities required during the visit of a dignitary/dignitaries or a delegation

does not require planning permission if:

- they are provided by, or on behalf of, STATE AUTHORITIES.

These structures MUST be removed after the visit of the dignitary/dignitaries or delegation for whom they were initially erected and the lands returned to their original condition

### 1.3.5 Class 20 – Temporary Use of a Premises During an Election or Referendum

The use of any premises in connection with the following does not require planning permission:

- Presidential elections;
- Dáil elections;
- European Parliament elections;
- Local Authority or Údarás na Gealtachta elections;
- Referendums – see the Referendum Act of 1942 for the definition of a Referendum.

The limitation on this "temporary" use is that it must discontinue after a maximum of 30 days.

# 1.4  Industrial Developments[1]

## 1.4.1  Class 21 – Various Types of Industrial Development

The following works are exempt from planning permission provided they are carried out by an "industrial undertaking" (*i.e.* a factory or business) on land already used by that business as it carries out its work, subject to the conditions/limitations listed below.

This exemption ALSO APPLIES to development on land used as a DOCK, HARBOUR OR QUAY where it is used by an "industrial undertaking".

Works exempt from planning permission include the provision, re-arranging, replacing or maintaining of:

- "private ways" (*i.e.* a private road);
- private railways, sidings or conveyors;
- sewers;
- mains;
- pipes;
- cables or other apparatus; and
- the erection or installation of plant, machinery, or "structures of the nature of plant or machinery" (*i.e.* anything similar).

Providing a hard surface area in connection with the industrial process carried out in the building is also exempt provided that it is located within the premises. This may allow for the storage of raw materials, for example, but is unlikely to allow for car parking as the key phrase is "an industrial process".

The exemption from planning permission applies to both plant and machinery that are either "replacements" or "additions" to existing structures.

**Limitations on Class 21**

The exemption is limited in the following ways:

- Development SHALL NOT CHANGE the EXTERNAL APPEARANCE of the premises. This is likely to be the most significant restraint on obtaining any benefit from this exemption as most works to industrial buildings change their appearance. The debate in this instance is likely to centre on whether the change is visible from a public area and whether any change has a material impact.

---

[1] An important consideration for industrial developments is where an exempted development may alter an overall building/site in such a way as to create a risk under the Major Accident Hazards section of the Planning regulations. In such cases the exemption does not apply. Given this, it is advisable that all industrial development proposals are checked with the Planning Authority or a Chartered Planner prior to commencing work. (See apendix 2B.)

- The HEIGHT of any new/replacement plant or machinery/structure CANNOT exceed 15m OR the height of the plant/machinery being replaced (whichever is greater); *e.g.* if the plant/structure being replaced is 20m in height then the replacement can be built to this height without planning permission. If the plant/structure being introduced is new then it can only be built to a maximum height of 15m without planning permission.

**Note:**

(a) Development should be considered on a "case by case" basis before seeking to avail of any benefit under this class of exemption. Restrictions established by the terms and conditions of any planning permission should also be considered in this case.

(b) This exemption does not apply where a Special Area Amenity Order is in effect (see Appendix 2).

## 1.4.2 Class 22 – Storing Necessary Industrial Materials on Site

Class 22 applies to the storage of materials within the grounds (curtilage) of an industrial building.

Planning permission is not required where materials being stored are USED IN CONNECTION with the industrial process being carried out in the building. The materials which may be stored include:

- raw materials;
- packing material;
- products;
- fuel; and
- deposits of waste resulting from the production / industrial process.

To be exempt, however, the raw material, packaging, fuel, product or waste MUST NOT BE VISIBLE FROM ANY PUBLIC ROAD.

Practical examples of this exemption include the following:

- "Fireclay" may be stored at a brickworks factory as it is a "raw material" used in the process.
- Wooden "off-cuts" may be stored outside a furniture factory as "waste" arising from the process.

However, these materials should not be seen from a public road as they may be considered to be in breach of the conditions and limitations of the exemption.

**Note:**

This exemption does not apply where a Special Area Amenity Order is in effect (see Appendix 2).

### 1.4.3    Class 23 – Certain Types of Development by Rail Companies

Most development carried out by a rail company (*e.g.* Irish Rail) does not require planning permission where:

- it is located ON, IN, UNDER or OVER LAND required in connection with the MOVEMENT OF RAIL TRAFFIC;
- this land is in operational use (*e.g.* land currently used by the rail company).

Development by a rail company does require planning permission when the work involves the construction, erection or development of:

- a railway bridge;
- a railway station;
- a residential structure;
- an office;
- a manufacturing or repair building/structure ("which is not situated wholly within the interior of a railway station"); or
- a car park of more that 60 spaces.

Planning permission is also required when the work involves the reconstruction or removal of any of the above structures in a manner that would materially change its appearance.

### 1.4.4    Class 24 – Works Carried Out by a Harbour Authority

Development carried out by a harbour authority does not require planning permission if:

- it is work carried out under the provisions of a "harbour works order" (see section 134 of the Harbours Act 1946).

These works MUST INVOLVE the construction, reconstruction, removal or extension of:

- docks;
- graving docks;
- quays;
- wharves;
- jetties;
- piers;
- embankments;
- breakwaters;
- roads;
- viaducts;
- tramways; or
- railways or aerodromes.

These works MUST NOT INVOLVE the construction or erection of:

- sheds;
- transit sheds;
- transhipment sheds;
- silos;
- stores; or
- other structures.

The reconstruction, or alteration, of any of the above structures that do not benefit from this exemption requires planning permission IF IT MATERIALLY ALTERS THE DESIGN OR EXTERNAL APPEARANCE of the structure. Minor changes to the external appearance are unlikely to require planning permission. Hovever, any such changes should be checked with the planning authority beforehand.

Also exempt from planning permission are:

- the cleaning, scouring, dredging, deepening or improving of a harbour, or harbour approaches, by its harbour authority;
- the removal of any obstructions within the harbour's limits; and
- the dumping of dredged sludge on land "zoned"/identified for this purpose in the local Development Plan for the area.

**Note:**

Where any changes to the external appearance of a building/structure are proposed, one should always check with the Planning Authority prior to commencing construction to see if they consider the work to be exempt from planning permission.

## 1.4.5 Class 25 – Development by An Bord Gais (The Irish Gas Board)

There are a series of exemptions in the planning regulations that allow for the development, without planning permission, of elements of gas transmission networks.

These exemptions allow, under certain circumstances, for the development of:

- underground pipelines for gas;
- mains, pipes, cables or other apparatus;
- cathodic protection equipment; and
- marker posts.

The above is only a general list of the various types of development that may be exempt from planning permission. Such development is, however, restricted by the Gas Act and exempted development varies depending on which section of the Gas Act approved/permitted the proposed development.

**Note:**

Only development allowed/approved under:

- section 8 or 40 of the Gas Act 1976; or
- section 2 of the Gas (Amendment) Act 1987

has the possibility of obtaining some benefit from this class of exemption.

**Note:**

(a) Ancillary development above ground associated with the works outlined earlier will generally require planning permission.

(b) It advisable to check any proposal with the Planning Authority prior to commencement.

(c) It is advisable to read the provisions of this class of exemption in the planning regulations in association with the various Gas Act and Gas (Amendment) Act provisions mentioned therein.

### 1.4.6   Class 26 – Development by Electricity Companies - Underground Cables

Class 26 allows for any "electricity undertaking" to carry out the following without planning permission:

- laying mains underground;
- laying pipes underground;
- laying cables underground;
- laying "other apparatus" underground.

**Note:**

(a) This is a very wide-ranging exemption. The Planning Authority should be consulted prior to commencing works/development as to whether or not it considers any such "pipe laying" exempt under this class.

(b) While planning authorities actively promote the development of underground cabling for electricity transmission, the question must be asked as to what limitations can be placed on this exemption.

(c) A definition of an "electricity undertaking" needs to be considered carefully with future changes to the electricity generation market. For example, is a private wind-farm an "electricity undertaking"?

### 1.4.7   Class 27 – Development by Electricity Companies – Power Lines

The development or construction by an "electricity undertaking" of:

- overhead power lines that will transmit/distribute power not exceeding 20 kV

does not require planning permission.

This basically applies to domestic type power lines that are common throughout urban areas.

**Note:**

(a) Also see Class 28 for power lines that have been granted planning permission.

(b) There appears to be no restriction in the planning regulations on the height/design of any poles erected for 20 kV power lines.

(c) This exemption does not apply where a Special Amenity Area Order is in effect (see Appendix 2).

(d) This exemption could be "de-exempted" if development takes place in an area where it may interfere with the character of the landscape (see Appendix 2). However, Article 9 of the 2001 Planning Regulations limits this restriction where the development consists only of the construction of an overhead line or cable not exceeding 100m in length for the purpose of conducting electricity from a distribution or transmission line to any premises (see Appendix 2),

### 1.4.8    Class 28 – The Location of an Overhead Power Line Granted Planning Permission

Where power lines do require planning permission, electricity companies are allowed a degree of freedom in the location/alignment of those lines.

If planning permission is granted, the Class 28 exemption allows:

● the development of AN OVERHEAD POWER LINE, not more than 40m from the alignment on which it was granted planning permission.

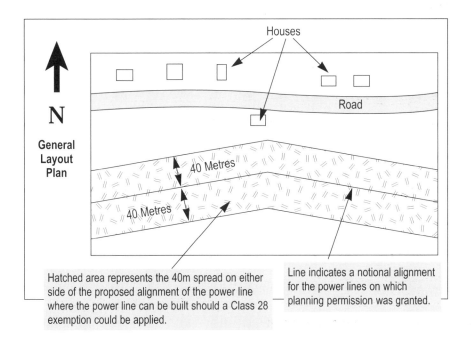

This exemption effectively means that the ESB can develop a power line along a corridor that is 80m wide.

This does not apply where a planning authority restricts the proposed alignment of a power line by a condition of the planning permission requiring it to follow a certain route, nor does it affect the property rights of adjoining landowners.

**Note:**
   (a) This exemption does not apply if the proposed power line is restricted by the terms and conditions of a planning permission.
   (b) This exemption does not apply where a Special Amenity Area Order is in effect (see Appendix 2).

### 1.4.9   Class 29 – Development by Electricity Companies – Substations

Class 29 allows for the development of substations for the distribution of electricity not exceeding 20 kV without planning permission. The only restriction is that:

● the volume of the substation shall not exceed 11 cub. m above ground level (measured externally).

It should be noted that ancillary to the development of such substations are works such as walls and gates. These may be exempted under another part of the Planning Regulations such as Class 11.

**Note:**

This exemption does not apply where a Special Amenity Area Order is in effect (see Appendix 2).

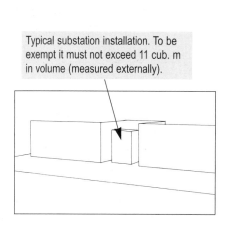

Typical substation installation. To be exempt it must not exceed 11 cub. m in volume (measured externally).

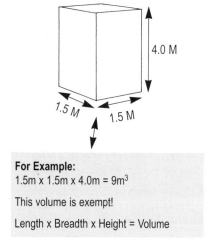

4.0 M

1.5 M    1.5 M

**For Example:**
1.5m x 1.5m x 4.0m = 9m$^3$

This volume is exempt!

Length x Breadth x Height = Volume

## 1.4.10   Class 30 – Development by An Post

Certain developments by An Post do not require planning permission under Class 28 of the Planning Regulations. Developments that are exempt include:

- pillarboxes, or other forms of letter boxes;
- road-side boxes for mail delivery;
- deposit boxes for the temporary storage of mail for local delivery; and
- machines that supply stamps/printed postage labels.

The implication of Class 28 is that An Post does not require planning permission for the development of basic elements of the postal system, *i.e.* post boxes, stamp machines and storage boxes.

## 1.4.11   Class 31 – Authorised Telecom Providers

Class 31 provides telecommunications providers with a wide range of exemptions from planning permission.

The Class 31 exemptions allow development without planning permission for the following:

- underground telecommunication structures or works;
- underground mains or cables;
- installing "any apparatus or equipment" underground;
- overhead telecommunications lines, *i.e.* phone lines, providing the poles they are on do not exceed 10m in height;
- poles carrying other telecommunication antennae can also be erected without planning permission where they are in place of a pole route that would otherwise have to be erected to carry overhead wires; do not exceed 10m in height and 0.6m in diameter; and carry either one transmitting or receiving dish (diameter not wider than 0.3m), one panel antenna (no longer than 0.5m, no wider than 0.3m or no deeper than 0.2m) and the field strength of the antenna/dish does not exceed limits specified by the Director of Telecommunication Regulation;
- telephone kiosks in a public place (these must have the written consent of the owners and occupiers of houses, or the "curtilage" of houses, located within 10m of the proposed kiosk location;
- satellite transmitting or receiving equipment (this cannot be higher than 10m; have antennae wider than 2m; be within 10m of a house boundary without the owner's consent; or be within 10m of a window of a "workroom" of any other building);
- permanent telecommunications exchanges or radio station containers (these cannot be more than 10m long, 3m wide or 3m tall; cannot be within 10m of a house boundary without the owner's written consent; or be within 10m of a window of a "workroom" of any other building);
- cabinets that are part of a telecommunications system (the volume of which cannot exceed 1.5 cub.m);

- radio links that can be transported cannot exceed 15m in height or 2m in width. They can only be used to provide for additional coverage at sporting, social or other events and they can be in place not more than two weeks before the event or more than eight weeks after the event. Temporary structures can also be allowed to demonstrate the visual effects of a telecommunications facility or to measure its output. In such cases it cannot be in place for more than 12 weeks without planning permission. They can also be allowed as a temporary replacement for a structure that is temporarily out of use due to an accident or another problem, but, again, shall not be in place for more than 12 weeks. In all cases the Planning Authority must be notified in writing before the temporary structures become operational;

- attaching mobile phone antennae to an existing antennae support structure used in connection with radio transmission or reception. This does not require planning permission where the number of antennae do not exceed 12 (no more than eight dish-type antennae can be attached and this is included in the total of 12); the antennae size cannot exceed the greatest size of the existing attached corresponding antennae type or in other cases 1.5m (l) x 0.4m (w) x 0.15m (d) for "panel type" antennae; 5.0m (l) x 0.10m (dia.) for "co-linear antennae"; or 1.8m (dia.) for dish antennae, or the size of existing antennae attached to the mast if they are smaller than the above; ionizing radiation emissions shall not exceed any limitations specified by the Director of Telecommunication Regulation; attachment to a platform can be carried out where one already exists and the height of the existing structure must not be exceeded;

- an existing antennae support structure may be replaced when this occurs no more than four weeks after its removal; the new structure must not exceed the previous one in height; the width of the replacement structure may not exceed the previous structure except where this was 2m or less; in such cases the width of the replacement structure can be up to twice that of the original, *e.g.* a 1.5m wide structure can be replaced by a 3.0m wide structure; the replacement structure cannot have an antennae support platform if the original structure did not; only the same number of antennae can be included on the replacement structure as on the original structure plus an additional 12 (see above) where they are mobile phone antennae; the dimensions of the replacement antennae cannot exceed the dimensions of those on the structure being replaced; any additional antennae cannot exceed the greatest dimensions of the "corresponding type" of the structure being replaced otherwise the sizes cannot exceed 1.5m (l) x 0.4m (w) x 0.15m (d) for "panel type" antennae; 5.0m (l) x 0.10m (dia.) for "co-linear antennae"; or 1.8m (dia.) for dish antennae; ionizing radiation emissions shall not exceed limitations specified by the Director of Telecommunication Regulation. The structure to be replaced can remain operational and in place during the construction of the replacement structure to maintain the integrity of the network; the replacement structure cannot be located more than 20m from the original structure;

- Antennae for high capacity transmission links can be erected without planning permission where only a dish type antennae is used for point to point communication; the additional antennae shall not exceed the design capacity of the existing structure; the only additional element that can be attached to the structure are brackets or other means of fixing the dish to the structures;

the dish cannot exceed the width of the support structure at the point where it is attached; the Planning Authority for the area must be notified in writing at least four weeks before the dish is proposed to be attached; ionizing radiation emissions shall not exceed limitations specified by the Director of Telecommunication Regulation;

- Antennae can be attached to the roofs, façades, chimneys or chimney pots or vent pipes of existing public or commercial buildings (not educational, childcare or hospital facilities), telegraph poles, lamp posts, flag poles, CCTV poles or electricity pylons without planning permission where the antennae is attached directly to the structure (not by way of a supporting structure); a structure with a flat roof can have a supporting fixture but this must not exceed the height of the parapet or railing of the roof by more than 2m, and access to the roof is only available to persons authorised by the Telecoms company. Where the antenna is attached to the façade of a building, a chimney or vent, it must match their colour in order to blend in. An antenna can be located in a chimney pot but must not protrude above the top of the pot; a new pot more suited to an antenna can be erected in place of an existing one but must be the same size, shape and colour as the original. The Planning Authority for the area must be notified in writing at least four weeks before the dish is proposed to be attached; ionizing radiation emissions shall not exceed limitations specified by the Director of Telecommunication Regulation.

**Note:**

(a) These exemptions allow for a wide range of works without planning permission by appropriately licensed telecommunications providers.

(b) The exemptions relating to mobile phone masts are particularly complex and professional advice should always be obtained on whether or not any such developments require planning permission.

(c) This exemption does not apply where a Special Area Amenity Order is in effect (see Appendix 2) except where the works proposed involve developing underground telecommunication structures or works, underground mains or cables, or installing "any apparatus or equipment" underground.

(d) With regard to mobile phone masts, the original planning permission is very important, as conditions may have been attached limiting the number of antennae or size of the structure.

## 1.4.12   Class 32 - Aerodromes

Class 32 provides those with an aerodrome licence (see the Irish Aviation Authority Aerodromes and Visual Ground Aids Order 1998) the right to carry out certain development including:

- the construction or erection of an airport operational building.

This exemption is subject to the following conditions:

- The development must be located within an airport.
- If the building has not been extended previously the floor area of the extension shall not exceed 500 sq. m or 15 per cent of the floor area of the building (whichever is smaller). For example, if the building has a floor area of 1,000 sq. m then it can only have a 150 sq. m extension.
- If the building has been extended before then the combined floor area of all extensions (existing and proposed) shall not exceed 500 sq. m or 15 per cent of the original floor area of the building (whichever is smaller).
- The Planning Authority for the area shall be notified of the proposed development no less than four weeks before the development takes place.

Also exempt under Class 32 are:

- Constructing, erecting, extending, altering or removing aprons, taxiways or airside roads used for aircraft movement, distribution of vehicles and equipment airside within the airport.
- Constructing, erecting or altering visual navigation aids and other ground / guidance features.
- Constructing, erecting or altering security fencing, gates, security cameras and other security infrastructure within an airport.
- Erecting or altering direction/warning signs within an airport.

# 1.5 Amenity and Recreational Developments

## 1.5.1 Class 33 – Development of Shrines, Parks and Sports Pitches

Under Class 33, the following developments do not require planning permission:

- developing private land as a park, private open space or ornamental garden;
- developing a roadside shrine (it cannot have a site area of more than 2 sq. m or a height that is 2m or more above the centre of the road next to or facing it). The shrine cannot be illuminated without planning permission;
- developing land for use for athletics or any other sport WHERE THERE IS NO CHARGE FOR ENTRY TO THE LAND. This does not include developing land for use as a golf course, pitch and putt course, shooting firearms, or as a venue for motor sport or aircraft.

**Note:**

This exemption does not apply to laying out lands for athletics or sports where no charge is payable by members of the public on lands where a Special Amenity Area Order is in effect (see Appendix 2).

## 1.5.2 Class 34 – Golf Courses and Pitch and Putt Courses

Under Class 34 certain development/works carried out at a Golf Course do not require planning permission. These include:

- works incidental to the maintenance and management of the golf course (or pitch and putt course); and
- alterations to the layout.

**Note:**

The exemption does not apply to an extension to the area of the golf course or pitch and putt course. This exemption may present difficulties in operation as a number of golf courses have been granted planning permission in accordance with a set of application drawings submitted to the Planning Authority. In this respect, the alteration of the layout may be considered a breach of the permission and, as such, it would be advisable to obtain professional advice or check any proposals with the Planning Authority beforehand.

## 1.5.3 Class 35 – Development associated with Waterways, Canals, Inland Waterways and Rivers

The exemptions offered under Class 35 would normally be used by the Office of Public Works in the course of the maintenance and improvement of inland waterways.

Development does not require planning permission if it involves the maintenance, improvement, reconstruction or restoration OF ANY OF THE FOLLOWING:

- a watercourse;
- a canal;
- a lock;
- a quay;
- a mooring;
- a harbour;
- a pier;
- a dry-dock;
- a river;
- a lake or other inland waterway or structure associated with the waterway; or
- any development incidental/associated with works on the above.

Also exempt from planning permission is the construction/erection of facilities generally associated with either the operation, use or management of either an inland waterway, canal, river, lake or watercourse. Structures constructed/erected for the benefit of the above cannot have:

- a floor area greater than 40 sq. m;
- a height greater than 6m if it is a building with a pitched roof;
- a height greater than 3m if it does not have a pitched roof, *i.e.* a flat-roofed structure;
- more than 24 car parking spaces (if the development is a car park).

**Note:**

The exemption can only be used by a "statutory undertaker", or a developer acting on their behalf, when carrying out works.

### 1.5.4   Class 36 – Development of Public Parks and Nature Reserves

**Parks**

Under Class 36, development ON LANDS USED AS A PUBLIC PARK, either by or on behalf of state authorities or other public bodies, *i.e.* local authorities, does not require planning permission where it involves providing, erecting or constructing structure(s) necessary/incidental to the MANAGEMENT OR OPERATION of any such park if that "structure" provided is incidental to the enjoyment of the park, or its use as an amenity.

However, such a structure cannot have:

- a floor area greater than 40 sq. m;
- a height greater than 10m (different heights for flat or pitched roofs are not specified);

- more than 40 car parking spaces if the development is a car park.

This exemption also allows development incidental to the use of the park to be carried out. This would normally be taken as meaning routine maintenance, etc.

### Reserves

Also exempted from planning permission under Class 36 is development ON A NATURE RESERVE of structures/works that are necessary/incidental TO THE MANAGEMENT or OPERATION of the NATURE RESERVE, or its ENJOYMENT.

- The provision, erection or construction of structures on Nature Reserves does not require planning permission provided it complies with the terms of the exemption.
- The development must be carried out by or on behalf of the Commissioners of Public Works.
- The NATURE RESERVE must have been established in accordance with section 15 of the Wildlife Act 1976 (as amended by the Wildlife (Amendment) Act 2000) for any development on it to be exempt from planning permission under Class 36.

However, any such structure cannot have:

- a floor area greater than 40 sq. m;
- a height greater than 10m (different heights for flat or pitched roofs are not specified);
- more than 40 car parking spaces if the development is a car park.

## 1.5.5    Class 37 – Funfairs and Bazaars

Caution should be used when seeking exemption from planning permission under Class 37. The exemption states that planning permission may not be required for any of the following:

- a fair;
- a funfair;
- a bazaar;
- a circus.

Or for the use of land for any local event that is in character:

- religious;
- cultural;
- educational;
- political;
- social;
- recreational; or
- sporting.

Along with the placement/use/maintenance of any temporary/movable structures in connection with the above, the use of land for local events does not require planning permission subject to the condition that the land on which the event/development takes place:

- SHALL NOT be used for more that 15 days continuously; and

- SHALL NOT be used for more than 30 days in total during the year.

**Note:**

Licensing procedures for many events are now in place under the Planning and Development Act 2000.

**Key Phrase**

The most important phrase in this exemption is LOCAL EVENT. Whether or not a development can be exempted under this Class is likely to stand or fall on the interpretation of LOCAL EVENT.

A very important factor in proving that an event is local would be where it is to be advertised.

# 1.6 Miscellaneous Development

## 1.6.1 Class 38 – Flags, Banners, National Emblems and their Support Structures

Putting up:

- flags;
- banners;
- national emblems; or
- structures for any of the above (*i.e.* flagpoles)

does not require planning permission if they:

- are located on a "State Authority" or EU Institution property/land.
- are located on property/land under the control of a "State Authority" or EU Institution.
- are on a building owned or controlled by a "State Authority" or EU Institution, or are within the building's boundary.

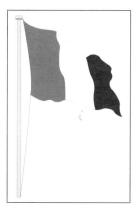

Putting up a flag pole on a State Authority property does not require planning permission.

This exemption releases STATE AUTHORITIES from the obligation to obtain planning permission for developments such as flag poles, flags and national emblems.

## 1.6.2 Class 39 – Providing a Lighthouse, Beacon, Buoy or Navigation Aids

The placing, keeping or erection of any:

- lighthouse;
- buoy;
- beacon; or
- other navigation aid to assist in air or sea navigation

does not require planning permission if it does not exceed 40m in height.

**Note:**

(a) There does not appear to be any restriction in this exemption on who may provide the beacon, lighthouse or navigation aid.

(b) This exemption does not apply where a Special Amenity Area Order is in effect (see Appendix 2).

### 1.6.3    Class 40 – Incidental Works (Burial Grounds, School Yards, Churchyard, Monument, Markets and Fairgreens)

Works incidental to the ongoing maintenance and use of any:

- burial ground;
- school yard;
- churchyard;
- monument;
- market;
- fairgreen; or
- showground

do not require planning permission EXCEPT where those works involve:

- erecting or constructing ANY WALL, FENCE or GATE bounding or abutting a public road;
- erecting or constructing any building, except a stall or store, WHICH IS wholly enclosed within a market building (should this stall or store not be wholly enclosed it is likely to require planning permission);
- reconstructing or altering any building other than any stall or store WHICH IS wholly enclosed within a market building.

**Note:**

With regard to the latter two restrictions, section 4(1)(h) of the Planning and Development Act 2000 is relevant and should be considered when seeking to obtain any benefit under this exemption.

### 1.6.4    Class 41 – Works Incidental to the Provisions of Acts of the Oireachteas

Certain works carried out under the following Acts/Regulations do not require planning permission:

- section 34 Local Government (Sanitary Services) Act 1948, excluding the provision of any hut, chalet, building, road or hardstanding;
- works in accordance with a notice under section 12 of the Local Government (Water Pollution) Act 1977;
- works in accordance with a notice under section 26 of the Air Pollution Act 1987;
- works in accordance with the conditions of a Fire Certificate issued under Part III of the Building Control Regulations 1997 (BUT NOT the development of an external fire escape or water tank);
- any works, or the removal of any object, by a planning authority in accordance with the provisions of any law.

## 1.6.5  Class 42 – Bring Facilities

Development of land for use as a bring facility (*e.g.* a recycling centre) does not require planning permission as long as:

- no more than five receptacles are provided;
- the capacity of each one does not exceed 4.5 cub. metres;
- they are not located on a public road;
- they are not located within 50m of a house without the consent of the house owner or occupier.

## 1.6.6  Class 43 – Excavations (for Research and Discovery)

Any EXCAVATIONS carried out on the following for "research and discovery" do not require planning permission:

- any site, feature or object of geological interest;
- any site of archaeological or historical interest in accordance with a licence under section 26 of the National Monuments Act 1930.

**Note:**

This exemption could not be used as a justification for quarrying.

## 1.6.7  Class 44 – Domestic Water Supplies/Group Water Schemes

Carrying out CERTAIN WORKS in order to provide a domestic water supply, or a Group Water Scheme IN ACCORDANCE WITH A SCHEME APPROVED by the Minister for the Environment and Local Government/Local Authority (for the purpose of obtaining a grant), will not require planning permission.

Where such works are approved by the Minister for the Environment and Local Government or a Local Authority, the only works EXEMPT FROM PLANNING PERMISSION are:

- sinking a well;
- drilling a borehole;
- erecting a pump;
- building a pumphouse; and
- "other works" required for providing domestic/group water supply.

**Note:**

(a) The basic implication of this exemption is that anything related to the provision of a domestic/Group Water Scheme does not require planning permission. However, given the scale of works generally involved in the provision of such schemes, it is advisable to consult with the Planning Authority prior to commencing works in order to determine whether any of the works are "de-exempted" through existing planning permissions or other restrictions on exemptions (identified in Appendix 2).

(b)  Group Water Schemes, and the works proposed as part of the scheme have occasionally been the subject of References to An Bord Pleanála as the scale of the works carried out have exceeded the scope of the exemption. It is, therefore, advisable to consult the Planning Authority prior to commencing works.

(c)  This exemption does not apply where a Special Amenity Area Order is in effect (see Appendix 2).

# 1.7 Various Minor Works

## 1.7.1 Class 45 – Drilling and Excavation

The following works do not require planning permission in certain circumstances:

- excavation;
- drilling.

To be exempt from planning permission, the above works MUST ONLY be for:

- surveying land;
- examining subsoil depth;
- examining subsoil conditions (called "subsoil nature" in the Regulations. This can relate to anything such as the soil composition and strata, for example).

This exemption DOES NOT APPLY to drilling and excavation that is carried out for the purposes of mineral exploration.

**Note:**
(a)  This exemption only refers to SUBSOIL.
(b)  See Class 5 of Part Three regarding exemptions for mineral exploration.

## 1.7.2 Class 46 – Structures (Measuring Waterflows and Volumes)

Structures or equipment built, or put in place, by:

- the Office of Public Works (Commissioners of Public Works);  ·
- the Environmental Protection Agency;
- Local Authorities "outside their functional area" (*i.e.* in some other local authority area)

FOR THE PURPOSE OF COLLECTING INFORMATION on the levels, flows, volumes of water in:

- rivers;
- watercourses;
- lakes;
- groundwaters

do not require planning permission.

**Note:**
(a)  The floor area of any building/structure provided for this purpose cannot be MORE THAN 8 sq. m in area, and its height cannot be MORE THAN 4m.

(b)  This exemption also includes development that occurs as a result of (*i.e.* incidental to) the development of any structure for the purpose of collecting information on levels, flows and volumes of water in the listed locations.

### 1.7.3    Class 47 – Structures (Measuring Air Quality)

Structures or equipment built, or put in place, by:

- the Environmental Protection Agency; or
- Local Authorities "outside their functional area" (*i.e.* in some other local authority area)

OF ANY EQUIPMENT OR STRUCTURE FOR THE PURPOSE OF COLLECTING INFORMATION on:

- air quality;
- the levels of pollutants in the atmosphere;
- the constituents (make up) of the atmosphere

do not require planning permission (any ancillary development related to the above also does not require planning permission).

**Note:**
(a)  Any equipment installed on an existing building must not protrude more than 2m in front of the building line nor go more than 2m above the height of the roof's ridgeline.
(b)  The floor area of any building/structure provided for this purpose cannot be MORE THAN 20 sq. m in area, and its height cannot be MORE THAN 3m.

### 1.7.4    Class 48 – Connections to Services (Various)

The CONNECTION of any premises (*i.e.* building or dwelling) to any of the following does not require planning permission:

- a "wired broadcast relay service", *e.g.* phones lines;
- a sewer;
- a watermain;
- a gas main; or
- an ESB line or cable.

**Note:**
(a)  Digging up the street or other lands is exempt from planning permission for the above purpose if it is to allow for any of the above connections. This exemption does not specify a difference between publicly owned lands and privately owned lands. In the case of private land, the owner's consent should be obtained; in the case of public land, a wayleave from the local authority may be necessary.
(b)  In the case of sewers and watermains, connection charges are normally required by the local authority.

## 1.7.5   Class 49 – Telecommunications Cabinets

The construction or erection of any cabinet to be used as part of a "wired broadcast relay service" (*e.g.* a phone system) does not require planning permission if:

- it is carried out by a person licensed under the Wireless Telegraphy (Wired Broadcast Relay Licence) Regulations 1974;
- has a volume (measured externally) of no more than 1 cub. m.

## 1.7.6   Class 50 – Demolition of Structures

The demolition of any building or structure does not require planning permission UNLESS:

- it is a habitable house (a house that is currently being lived in or was last used as a dwelling – see Appendix 3 for the planning definition of "habitable house");
- it is a building that is part of a terrace of buildings;
- it is a building that abuts another building in separate ownership.

### Houses

The only time that PART of a habitable house can be demolished is:

- when the demolition is necessary to provide for the development of a porch or extension exempted under the Regulations (see Classes 1 and 7); or
- when the demolition is in accordance with a planning permission that has been granted.

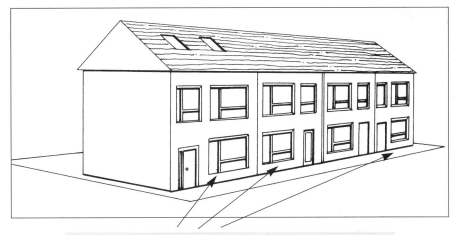

None of the above can be demolished without planning permission as they are all:

- abutting buildings in separate ownership;
- in a terrace;
- houses that are lived in.

**Note:**

(a) This exemption basically means that MOST BUILDINGS can be demolished without planning permission.

(b) IT IS IMPORTANT TO NOTE that this exemption is MOST DEFINITELY restricted by the Regulations. For example, if the property proposed to be demolished is a protected structure in either the Development Plan or Draft Development Plan for the area, you cannot obtain any benefit from this exemption. See Appendix 2 – Protected Structures.

(c) Demolition under this exemption does not apply where a Special Amenity Area Order is in effect (see Appendix 2).

## 1.7.7   Class 51 – Commissioners of Public Works (Works by)

The carrying out of any works by the Commissioners of Public Works for:

- the maintenance of works/structures for which the Commissioners are responsible under the Arterial Drainage Act 1945, or any order made under that Act; or
- any development that is incidental to those works

does not require planning permission.

## 1.7.8   Class 52 – Development by a Regional Fisheries Board

Class 52 exempts development by the Regional Fisheries Boards from planning permission if that development consists of any of the following:

- a footbridge (not more than 1.2m wide or 8m long);
- a fish pass;
- a fish screen or barrier;
- a walkway (not more than 1.2m wide);
- a fishing stand (not more than 10 sq. m in area); or
- a fish counter.

## 1.7.9   Class 53 – Development below the High Water Mark

Class 53 exempts development below the High Water Mark carried out in accordance with a licence under the Fisheries (Amendment) Act 1997 or one deemed to be granted under that Act or the Fisheries or Foreshore (Amendment) Act,1998.

## 1.7.10  Class 54 – Reclaiming Land from the Foreshore

Class 54 exempts the reclamation of areas not more than 100 sq. m from the foreshore if the development is to be for any of the following purposes:

- protecting a pier;
- protecting a slipway; or
- protecting some other structure on the foreshore.

## 1.7.11   Class 55 – Satellite Dishes on Business Premises

Class 55 exempts the placing of a satellite dish within the curtilage of a business premises for transmitting or receiving where:

- not more than one antenna is on the premises;
- the dish does not exceed 2m in diameter;
- the dish is not located on the front slope of the roof of the premises or higher than the highest part of the roof;
- the antenna is not located on or in front of the front wall of the premises.

## 1.7.12   Article 10 Exemptions – Bed and Breakfasts, Construction of Shops and Restaurants by a State Authority

Under Article 10 of the planning regulations certain developments are exempt from planning permission. These are as follows.

### Bed and Breakfasts

Planning permission is not required for the use of no more than four bedrooms in a house as overnight guest accommodation FOR NOT MORE THAN FOUR PERSONS.

### Note:

This must not contravene any conditions attached to a planning permission nor be inconsistent with any specified use. Conditions attached to planning permissions restricting this exemption are becoming more common in certain parts of Ireland.

### Development of Shops and Restaurants by a State Authority

Where a State Authority develops a shop or restaurant for the visiting public in a building controlled or occupied by a State Authority, no planning permission is required.

### Childminding

The use of a house for childminding is exempt from planning permission. Childminding is defined in the Regulations as minding no more than six children, including the children, if any, of the person minding, in the house of that person, for profit or gain.

### Environmental Protection Agency – Certain Works Necessary Due to EPA Requirements

Certain works that are necessary due to the requirements of either an Integrated Pollution Control Licence issued under the Environmental Protection Agency Act 1990 or a Waste Licence issued under the provisions of the Waste Management Act 1996 are exempt from the requirement to obtain planning permission.

### Building Regulations

Development (not development consisting of the development of a building designed to cater for two or more separate dwellings) necessary to secure compliance with the 1997 Building Regulations shall be exempt from the need to obtain planning permission where the permission was granted before June 1, 1992.

## Drainage Schemes

Works specified under a drainage scheme confirmed by the Minister for Finance under Part II of the Arterial Drainage Act 1945 or the Arterial Drainage (Amendment) Act 1995 carried out by, on behalf of, or in partnership with the Commissioners for Public Works shall be exempt from planning permission.

## State Developments

Certain security works can be carried out without planning permission under Article 86 of the Planning Regulations. While this is still development it is excluded from the public notice procedures that apply to most State developments and therefore can be put in place without notice to the general public. In summary, this work applies to the following:

- Works carried out in the interests of national security within or bounding any building or installation controlled or occupied by a State Authority (but not structures such as Garda Stations, Barracks, etc.).
- Security works within or bounding the home of a dwelling occupied by a holder or former holder of public office or any other public servant (or former public servant).
- Works carried out within or bounding the property of a person in receipt of protection from the Garda where such protection relates to the administration of justice.

# Chapter Two – Exemptions for Advertisements and Advertising Structures

This chapter addresses Part Two of the Second Schedule of the Local Government (Planning and Development) Regulations 2001. Part Two identifies exemptions from planning permission for advertisements and advertising structures.

This chapter seeks to simplify the often confusing advertising exemptions, providing a clear guide to the various types of exemption and an interpretation of their content. As with Chapter One each "Class" of the Exemptions shall be addressed in the same order in which it occurs in the Planning Regulations.

## Part Two
### Advertisements and Advertising Structures

#### Important Notes:

***Advertisement*** - Defined in the Planning Acts as "any word, letter, model, balloon, kite, poster, notice, device or representation employed for the purpose of advertisement, announcement or direction".

***Advertisement Structure*** - Defined in the Planning Acts as "any structure which is a hoarding, scaffold, framework, pole, standard, device or sign (whether illuminated or not) and which is used or intended for use for exhibiting advertisements".

***Advertisements in Gaeltacht areas*** - Where an advertisement is proposed to be located in a Gaeltacht area under the exempted development provisions it must be in Irish or Irish and other languages (with prominence given to Irish text) and have identical text in all languages.

# 2.1.1 Advertisements and Structures

## 2.1.1 Class 1 – Advertisements Exhibited on or Attached to any Business Premises

Signs exhibited on any BUSINESS PREMISES should not require planning permission IF THEY REFER TO the BUSINESS/ACTIVITY being carried out there, or the GOODS/SERVICES PROVIDED, IF THEY FOLLOW THE FORMULAS AND DESIGN GUIDES below for any one sign (or combination of signs) and do not come within the scope of the restrictions specified in Appendix 2.

The standards, conditions and limitations established under this Class One exemption do not apply to signs on business premises permitted under Class Two, Three or Five (see below). The exemptions generally apply to advertisements exhibited, attached or affixed to a building or a premises. Each of the specific exemptions is phrased to account for this, but it is advisable that the Planning Authority be consulted prior to erecting any signage.

### 2.1.1.1 Advertisements Located on the FRONT of a Business Premises

The area (in metres squared) of all signs located on the front of a premises that are exempt from the requirement to obtain planning permission is calculated by taking the length of the building front (in metres) x 0.3 - (minus) the area of existing signs exhibited on the premises BUT NOT attached to a building on the premises. The sign cannot be more than 4m above ground level and the combined area of all such signs to be attached to the property should not exceed 5 sq. m.

**Example**

*Question*: A business has a building/property with a 30m front wall, there is already a 3 sq. m sign on the premises but this is not attached to the building. The business wants to attach a 10 sq. m sign to the front of the building. Its height is 3.5m. Does this require planning permission?

*Answer*:   30 m x 0.3 = 9m$^2$ (-3m$^2$ of the existing sign) = 6m$^2$

This exceeds the 5 sq. m limit. Therefore, planning permission is necessary to put up a 10 sq. m sign.

### 2.1.1.2 Advertisements Located on ANY FACE of a Business Premises (excluding the Front of a Building)

The area of the advertisements shall not be greater than 1.2 sq. m in any case. The area of the illuminated portions of the advertisements cannot be greater than 0.3 sq. m. The advertisement cannot be more than 4m above ground level. It is most likely that the area limitations specified in this case would refer to combined signage.

### 2.1.1.3 Advertisements not Attached to ANY FACE of a Building but Located on the Premises

The area of the advertisements shall not be greater than 3.0 sq. m. The area of the illuminated portions of the advertisements cannot be greater than 1.5 sq. m. The advertisements cannot be more than 2.5m above ground level.

### 2.1.1.4 Design of Any Sign Exhibited

- Any advertisement (and the advertising structure) that projects over any part of a public road by more than 5cm (0.05m) must be at least 2m above the road level.
- Any advertisement (and the advertising structure) projecting more than 5cm over a public road cannot extend more than 1m over that road.
- Where an advertisement that projects more than 5cm over a public road IS CIRCULAR, its diameter shall not exceed 1m NOR shall any other advertisement be attached to it.
- Where an advertisement projects over the public road by more than 5cm from any external "face"/wall of a building (or from a swinging or fixed sign or some other form of advertising structure) and IT IS NOT CIRCULAR in shape, the area of the advertisement shall not exceed 1.2 sq. m OR, if there are a number of signs, they shall not have an individual area of more than 0.4 sq. m (*i.e.* three 0.4 sq. m signs).
- Any logo/symbol/device/model on any advertisement exempted under Class 1 shall not exceed 0.6m (60cms) in height without planning permission.
- Any lettering on an advertisement exempted under Class 1 shall not exceed 0.3m (30cms) in height without planning permission.
- An advertisement must not cover any part of a door or window.
- Where any advertisement or structure is attached to a building, its height cannot exceed 4m above ground without planning permission.
- Where any advertisement is not attached to a building or structure, its height cannot exceed 2.5m above ground without planning permission.

### Note: Restrictions on Class 1

(a) The restrictions on height of 2.5m above ground for advertisements not attached to a building and 4.0m above ground for advertisements attached to a building, above which planning permission is necessary, would appear to apply to all advertising signs or structures unless otherwise specified.

(b) The above exemptions do not apply where the advertisements or advertising structures are to be located on a building(s) identified as a Protected Structure or a Proposed Protected Structure in the Development Plan or any Draft Development Plan for the area where the proposed development is located (see Appendix 2).

(c) The above exemptions do not apply where the advertisements or advertising structures are to be located on the exterior of a building within an Architectural Conservation Area or an area specified in a Draft Development Plan or Development Plan as an Architectural Conservation Area (see Appendix 2).

(d) This exemption does not apply where a Special Amenity Area Order is in effect (see Appendix 2).

## 2.1.2   Class 2 – Advertisements Inside Shop Windows

Signs/advertisements proposed inside any shop window as part of a window display (the signs being visible from outside the shop window) do not require planning permission where the following formula is followed.

### 2.1.2.1   Formula:

The combined area of all advertisements visible through or fixed to the window should equal no more than 25 per cent of the area of the window.

Therefore, with a 10 sq. m window, only a maximum of 2.5 sq. m of advertising can be visible through it, or fixed to the inside of the window.

**Note:**
  (a)  This also applies to illuminated advertisements visible through (attached to the inside of) a shop window.
  (b)  The above exemptions do not apply where the advertisements or advertising structures are to be located on a building(s) identified as a Protected Structure or a Proposed Protected Structure in the Development Plan or any Draft Development Plan for the area where the proposed development is located (see Appendix 2).
  (c)  The above exemptions do not apply where the advertisements or advertising structures are to be located on the exterior of a building within an Architectural Conservation Area or an area specified in a Draft Development Plan or Development Plan as an Architectural Conservation Area (see Appendix 2).

## 2.1.3   Class 3 – Advertisements Located Inside a Business

Any advertisement that is located inside a business, and THAT CANNOT BE SEEN FROM OUTSIDE, does not require planning permission.

**Note:**
  (a)  The above exemptions do not apply where the advertisements or advertising structures are to be located on a building(s) identified as a Protected Structure or a Proposed Protected Structure in the Development Plan or any Draft Development Plan for the area where the proposed development is located (see Appendix 2).
  (b)  The above exemptions do not apply where the advertisements or advertising structures are to be located on the exterior of a building within an Architectural Conservation Area or an area specified in a Draft Development Plan or Development Plan as an Architectural Conservation Area (see Appendix 2).

## 2.1.4    Class 4 – Flags Used as Advertisements

A flag attached to AN UPRIGHT FLAGPOLE on top of a business does not require planning permission where:

- there is only one flag;
- the flag does not have any inscriptions on it;
- the flag ONLY has on it the name, "device" or logo of the business/person operating from the business premises;
- the flagpole is attached to the roof of the business and is upright.

**Note:**
(a) It may be maintained that the height of a flagpole attached to the roof of a business cannot exceed 4m above ground level due to the provisions of Class 1 and its height restrictions on advertisements attached to business premises. See Class 1.

(b) This exemption does not apply where a Special Amenity Area Order is in effect (see Appendix 2).

(c) The above exemptions do not apply where the advertisements or advertising structures are to be located on a building(s) identified as a Protected Structure or a Proposed Protected Structure in the Development Plan or any Draft Development Plan for the area where the proposed development is located (see Appendix 2).

(d) The above exemptions do not apply where the advertisements or advertising structures are to be located on the exterior of a building within an Architectural Conservation Area or an area specified in a Draft Development Plan or Development Plan as an Architectural Conservation Area (see Appendix 2).

## 2.1.5    Class 5 – "Brass Plates" at the Entrance to a Building/Advertisements at the Entrance to a Building or Premises

Businesses can put up advertisements or name plates, *i.e.* "brass plates", at the entrance to their property. These are only exempt from planning permission when:

- the area of the sign does not exceed 0.3 sq. m;
- only one is displayed at the entrance (or each entrance) per "business";
- the sign refers to a person, partnership or company carrying out a service, business or trade at the premises.

**Note:**
(a) If, for example, 10 businesses share the same building, each can erect a "Name Plate".

(b) Advertisements of this type can be located on a building(s) listed as a Protected Structure or Proposed Protected Structure in any Development Plan or Draft Development Plan for the area.

(c) Advertisements or advertising structures of this type located on the exterior of a building within an Architectural Conservation Area or an area specified in a Draft Development Plan or Development Plan as an Architectural Conservation Area are exempt.

### 2.1.6    Class 6 – Advertisements for Religious/ Recreational/Educational Events, Medical (or similar) Facilities, Guesthouses (or similar, but not a Hotel) for Overnight Accommodation/Public Houses/Blocks of Flats/Pubs/Boarding Houses or Hostels

Advertisements for any of the above do not require planning permission when:

- they are located on the land where the event/business that they advertise is located;
- they are not more than 0.6 sq. m in area;
- the advertisement or the advertising structure does not exceed 2.5m in height above ground level;
- no more than one advertisement is located on each road frontage. For example, if a B & B is located on a corner site, thereby having two "frontages", one advertisement can be erected on each frontage as per the above standards.

**Note:**

(a)   This exemption does not apply where a Special Amenity Area Order is in effect (see Appendix 2).

(b)   See Class 1.

(c)   The above exemptions do not apply where the advertisements or advertising structures are to be located on a building(s) identified as a Protected Structure or a Proposed Protected Structure in the Development Plan or any Draft Development Plan for the area where the proposed development is located (see Appendix 2).

(d)   The above exemptions do not apply where the advertisements or advertising structures are to be located on the exterior of a building within an Architectural Conservation Area or an area specified in a Draft Development Plan or Development Plan as an Architectural Conservation Area (see Appendix 2).

### 2.1.7    Class 7 – Advertisements on Enclosed Property

Any advertisement located on property that is enclosed, or almost enclosed by:

- walls;
- hedgerows;
- fences, etc., or
- a similar structure or screen;

does not require planning permission if:

- it cannot be "readily seen" from lands outside;
- the land on which the sign is located is not a public park area/public garden (area for public recreation/"enjoyment");

- the land on which the sign is located is not "enclosed land" used by a "railway undertaking".

**Note:**

(a) See Class 1.

(b) The above exemptions do not apply where the advertisements or advertising structures are to be located on a building(s) identified as a Protected Structure or a Proposed Protected Structure in the Development Plan or any Draft Development Plan for the area where the proposed development is located (see Appendix 2).

(c) The above exemptions do not apply where the advertisements or advertising structures are to be located on the exterior of a building within an Architectural Conservation Area or an area specified in a Draft Development Plan or Development Plan as an Architectural Conservation Area (see Appendix 2).

## 2.1.8 Class 8 – Advertisements in Bus/Railway Stations/Airports and Ferry Ports

Any advertisement in a Bus or Railway Station, Ferry Port or Airport THAT CANNOT BE SEEN FROM OUTSIDE THE PREMISES does not require planning permission. No restriction on the size of the advertisement is specified in the Planning Regulations.

**Note:**

(a) See Class 1.

(b) The above exemptions do not apply where the advertisements or advertising structures are to be located on a building(s) identified as a Protected Structure or a Proposed Protected Structure in the Development Plan or any Draft Development Plan for the area where the proposed development is located (see Appendix 2).

(c) The above exemptions do not apply where the advertisements or advertising structures are to be located on the exterior of a building within an Architectural Conservation Area or an area specified in a Draft Development Plan or Development Plan as an Architectural Conservation Area (see Appendix 2).

## 2.1.9 Class 9 – For Sale/Letting Signs (on Houses and Property)

Advertisements for the sale of Houses, Buildings, Property or Land (but not advertisements for the sale of an advertising structure) do not require planning permission when:

- they are on the property for sale or lease;
- their area does not exceed 0.6 sq. m for a house sale/lease;
- their area does not exceed 1.2 sq. m for any other structure, building or land sale or lease;

- there is only one on the property for sale or lease;
- they are taken down no more than seven days after the sale or lease.

**Note:**

(a) Advertisements of this type can be located on a building(s) listed as a Protected Structure or Proposed Protected Structure in any Development Plan or Draft Development Plan for the area.

(b) Advertisements or advertising structures of this type located on the exterior of a building within an Architectural Conservation Area or an area specified in a Draft Development Plan or Development Plan as an Architectural Conservation Area are exempt.

## 2.1.10 Class 10 – Advertisements for the Sale of Goods or Livestock

Advertisements for the sale of goods or livestock do not require planning permission when all of the following conditions are satisfied:

- The sign is located on lands where the sale is to take place, or the goods/livestock/animals, are located.
- The land is not normally/regularly used for such sales.
- The area of the advertisement does not exceed 0.6 sq. m.
- Only one sign is exhibited.
- The advertisement should be placed on the lands on the day of the sale or at some time preceding it.
- The sign is taken down no more than seven days after the sale.

**Note:**

(a) The above exemptions do not apply where the advertisements or advertising structures are to be located on a building(s) identified as a Protected Structure or a Proposed Protected Structure in the Development Plan or any Draft Development Plan for the area where the proposed development is located (see Appendix 2).

(b) The above exemptions do not apply where the advertisements or advertising structures are to be located on the exterior of a building within an Architectural Conservation Area or an area specified in a Draft Development Plan or Development Plan as an Architectural Conservation Area (see Appendix 2).

## 2.1.11 Class 11 – Advertisements for Building Works/Developments

Advertisements typically seen on building sites showing the development being constructed appear to be exempt under this Class Eleven exemption. They do not appear to require planning permission where the following conditions are satisfied:

- Where there is only one sign, its area should be less than 3.5 sq. m.
- Where there is only one sign, the height of that sign does not exceed 6m above ground level.
- When there is more than one sign, the area of each sign should not exceed 0.6 sq. m and the area of all such signs together should not exceed 3.5 sq. m.

- If there is more than one sign, the height of any one such sign shall not exceed 4.0m above ground level.
- The sign(s) must be taken down no more than seven days after the completion of the development.

**Note:**

(a) This exemption does not apply where a Special Area Amenity Order is in effect (see Appendix 2).

(b) The above exemptions do not apply where the advertisements or advertising structures are to be located on a building(s) identified as a Protected Structure or a Proposed Protected Structure in the Development Plan or any Draft Development Plan for the area where the proposed development is located (See Appendix 2).

(c) The above exemptions do not apply where the advertisements or advertising structures are to be located on the exterior of a building within an Architectural Conservation Area or an area specified in a Draft Development Plan or Development Plan as an Architectural Conservation Area (see Appendix 2).

## 2.1.12 Class 12 – Warning Signs

Warning/Direction/Announcement Signs exhibited/erected by a "Statutory Undertaker" announcing some event/works/development do not require planning permission when they concern some activity being carried out by that undertaker. For example, warning signs about construction works being carried out by a Local Authority would come under this class of exemption.

**Note:**

(a) There does not appear to be a restriction on the number of such signs in the Regulations.

(b) The above exemptions do not apply where the advertisements or advertising structures are to be located on a building(s) identified as a Protected Structure or a Proposed Protected Structure in the Development Plan or any Draft Development Plan for the area where the proposed development is located (see Appendix 2).

(c) The above exemptions do not apply where the advertisements or advertising structures are to be located on the exterior of a building within an Architectural Conservation Area or an area specified in a Draft Development Plan or Development Plan as an Architectural Conservation Area (see Appendix 2).

## 2.1.13 Class 13 – Warning/Identification/Direction Signs on a Premises

Advertisements that are placed on any property that are intended to either WARN, GIVE DIRECTIONS or IDENTIFY the property do not require planning permission when:

- their area does not exceed 0.3 sq. m.

**Note:**

(a) There does not appear to be a restriction on the number of such signs in the Regulations.

(b) The above exemptions do not apply where the advertisements or advertising structures are to be located on a building(s) identified as a Protected Structure or a Proposed Protected Structure in the Development Plan or any Draft Development Plan for the area where the proposed development is located (see Appendix 2).

(c) The above exemptions do not apply where the advertisements or advertising structures are to be located on the exterior of a building within an Architectural Conservation Area or an area specified in a Draft Development Plan or Development Plan as an Architectural Conservation Area (see Appendix 2).

### 2.1.14  Class 14 – Election Posters/Advertisements

Any advertisement/poster/advertising structure erected for a Presidential, Dáil, E.U. Parliament, Local Authority or Udarás na Gaeltachta election or Referendum does not require planning permission provided:

● the advertisements/posters/structures are be taken down at least seven days after the Election.

**Note:**

(a) The above exemptions do not apply where the advertisements or advertising structures are to be located on a building(s) identified as a Protected Structure or a Proposed Protected Structure in the Development Plan or any Draft Development Plan for the area where the proposed development is located (see Appendix 2).

(b) The above exemptions do not apply where the advertisements or advertising structures are to be located on the exterior of a building within an Architectural Conservation Area or an area specified in a Draft Development Plan or Development Plan as an Architectural Conservation Area (see Appendix 2).

### 2.1.15  Class 15 – Advertisements Required by Government Acts (Enactments)

Advertisements that are required as part of any Government enactment appear to be exempt from planning permission.

**Note:**

(a) It is advised that the full text of Class 15 is referred to in association with the relevant Government Act when any exemption under this class is considered.

(b) Advertisements of this type can be located on a building(s) listed for preservation/protection in any Development Plan or proposed to be listed in a Draft Development Plan for the area.

(c) Advertisements or advertising structures of this type located on the exterior of a building within an Architectural Conservation Area or an area specified in a Draft Development Plan or Development Plan as an Architectural Conservation Area are exempt.

### 2.1.16 Class 16 – Advertisements for Local Event

Any signs erected to advertise a LOCAL EVENT that is:

- religious;
- cultural;
- educational;
- sporting;
- political;
- social;
- recreational; or
- advertising "any temporary matter" associated with a local event such as the above, for example, a First Aid Station at a sporting event;

do not require planning permission where:

- the event is not carried out/promoted for commercial purposes;
- the signs do not exceed 1.2 sq. m in area;
- the signs are not erected above 2.5 sq. m above ground level;
- the advertisements are placed on an existing advertising structure only;
- the signs are taken down no more than seven days after the event.

**Note:**

(a) There is no restriction on the number of such signs that may be erected.

(b) This exemption should be read in conjunction with Class 17 (see below) which outlines exemptions from planning permission for advertising for specific uses such as funfairs, carnivals and travelling entertainment among others. Events catered for by Class 17 cannot obtain any benefit from exemption allowed under Class 16.

(c) The fact that the Planning Regulations state that the events cannot be carried out for commercial purposes would appear to be a severe restriction given that many local sporting/cultural events generally have an element of fundraising involved. As a result, it is advisable to consult the Local Authority in order to ascertain its view of what "commercial" implies.

(d) This exemption does not apply where an Special Amenity Area Order is in effect (see Appendix 2).

(e) The above exemptions do not apply where the advertisements or advertising structures are to be located on building(s) identified as a Protected Structure or a Proposed Protected Structure in the Development Plan or any Draft Development Plan for the area where the proposed development is located (see Appendix 2).

(f)   The above exemptions do not apply where the advertisements or advertising structures are to be located on the exterior of a building within an Architectural Conservation Area or an area specified in a Draft Development Plan or Development Plan as an Architectural Conservation Area (See Appendix 2).

### 2.1.17   Class 17 – Advertisements for Funfairs, Circuses, Carnivals, Shows, Musicians, Players or Travelling Entertainment

Advertisements/posters for any of the above do not require planning permission if the advertisements:

- are posters;
- are bills;
- are placards;
- do not exceed 1.2 sq. m;
- are placed on an existing advertising structure only;
- are not higher than 2.5m above ground level;
- are taken down no more than 7 days after the last performance to which they relate.

**Note:**

(a)   This exemption does not apply where a Special Amenity Area Order is in effect (see Appendix 2).

(b)   The above exemptions do not apply where the advertisements or advertising structures are to be located on a building(s) identified as a Protected Structure or a Proposed Protected Structure in the Development Plan or any Draft Development Plan for the area where the proposed development is located (see Appendix 2).

(c)   The above exemptions do not apply where the advertisements or advertising structures are to be located on the exterior of a building within an Architectural Conservation Area or an area specified in a Draft Development Plan or Development Plan as an Architectural Conservation Area (see Appendix 2).

### 2.1.18   Class 18 – Farming/Agricultural Demonstrations

Advertisements that refer to demonstrations of farming/agricultural methods or processes do not require planning permission if:

- only one advertisement is displayed on the land where the event takes place;
- the advertisement is located on the property where the event takes place;
- the sign does not exceed 0.6 sq. m in area;
- the advertisement is taken down no more than seven days after the event.

**Note:**

(a) Typically, such a sign could be taken as referring to a farming show, although it is likely that such events would exceed limitations on planning exemptions in many respects.

(b) The above exemptions do not apply where the advertisements or advertising structures are to be located on a building(s) identified as a Protected Structure or a Proposed Protected Structure in the Development Plan or any Draft Development Plan for the area where the proposed development is located (see Appendix 2).

(c) The above exemptions do not apply where the advertisements or advertising structures are to be located on the exterior of a building within an Architectural Conservation Area or an area specified in a Draft Development Plan or Development Plan as an Architectural Conservation Area (see Appendix 2).

# Chapter Three – Exemptions for Rural Developments

This chapter addresses Part Three of the Second Schedule to the Planning Regulations. Part Three provides exemptions from planning permission for rural developments.

As with the previous sections, each "Class" of the Exemptions shall be addressed in the same order in which it occurs in the Planning Regulations providing the most likely interpretation for each exception.

## Part Three

# 3.1 Camping

## 3.1.1 Class 1 – Camping Uses

The TEMPORARY use of any land for:

- any tent (the exemption specifically states tent, not "tents", therefore a camping site with a number of tents may require planning permission)
- the siting of a campervan/caravan used for camping;
- mooring any boat for the purpose of camping;
- mooring any barge or other vessel for the purpose of camping

does not require planning permission when:

- 100m separate any one tent or caravan from another tent or caravan;
- no tent, caravan, or boat ("vessel") can remain "on the land" for more than 10 days (placing the caravan on the land for more than 10 days would require planning permission);
- the tent, caravan or boat (vessel) cannot be used for any sale, storage or advertisement of goods;
- the tent, caravan or boat cannot be used for any business;
- no tent or caravan shall be within 50m of a public road unless it is enclosed by some wall/hedge etc. that has an average height of not lower than 1.5m.

**Note:**

This is a restrictive exemption that caters for individual campers and caravaners and not any commercial activity or traveller settlement.

## 3.1.2 Class 2 – Scouting Organisations

The TEMPORARY use of any land by a SCOUTING ORGANISATION does not require planning permission if that land use is:

- for a camp;
- used for any period or periods not exceeding 30 days in any year.

**Note:**

- (a) It is advisable that any prolonged period of use be cleared with the County Council prior to commencement.
- (b) This Class potentially provides an "escape clause" for scouting organisations from the restrictions of Class 1.

# 3.2 Minor Works

## 3.2.1 Class 3 – Watercourses and Associated Works

Works involving the CONSTRUCTION or MAINTENANCE of any:

- gully;
- drain;
- trough;
- pond;
- pit; or
- culvert

or works involving:

- deepening a watercourse;
- widening a watercourse;
- removing obstructions from watercourses;
- constructing ("making") or repairing any embankment when working on any of the above

do not require planning permission.

**Note:**
This exemption does not apply where a Special Amenity Area Order is in effect (see Appendix 2).

## 3.2.2 Class 4 – Fences or Walls

The construction of ANY FENCE OR WALL which IS BOUNDING ANY DWELLING, and is located in a rural area or is connected with farming, does not require planning permission where that fence or wall:

- does not exceed 3m if used in connection with deer farming or conservation;
- does not exceed 2m in all other cases;
- is not made from sheet metal (*i.e.* corrugated iron).

# 3.3  Mineral and Petroleum Prospecting

### 3.3.1  Class 5 – Prospecting (Minerals and Mining)

Any works carried out on lands, or structures erected to facilitate prospecting, do not require planning permission IF THEY RESULT FROM, and accord with, a PROSPECTING/EXPLORATION LICENCE issued by the Minister for Transport, Energy and Communications under the Minerals Acts, or Petroleum and Other Minerals Development Act.

**Note:**
- (a)  See Class 43 - Part One.
- (b)  See Class 45 - Part One.
- (c)  This exemption does not apply where a Special Amenity Area Order is in effect (see Appendix 2).
- (d)  It also allows for petroleum exploration under a "reserved area licence".

# 3.4 Agricultural Buildings and Land Reclamation

## 3.4.1   Class 6 – Roofed Structures Housing Animals

The provision of a roofed structure as housing for:

- cattle;
- sheep;
- goats;
- donkeys;
- horses;
- deer;
- rabbits

does not require planning permission when all of the following are satisfied:

- The floor area does not exceed 200 sq. m (if the structure being provided is an extension, the limit for the original building and its extension is 200 sq. m combined).
- The structure is only used for agricultural purposes.
- The floor area of the building proposed does not exceed 300 sq. m when considered together with other such existing structures in the same farmyard complex OR any such buildings within 100m of the complex where the building is to be located.
- Effluent storage shall be provided that is appropriate to the size, use and location of the structure proposed in line with the requirements of the Department of Agriculture, Food and Rural Development and Department of the Environment and Local Government.
- Water pollution by effluent shall be avoided.
- Effluent from the structure shall not be stored within 10m of a public road.
- The building proposed cannot be located within 10m of any public road.
- If the proposed building is located within 100m of the public road, its height cannot exceed 8m.
- The proposed building, or location for stored effluent from the building, shall not be located within 100m of a dwelling or "residential building", school, hospital, church or any building used for public "assembly" without the consent of the owner/occupier/person in charge of that property.
- No unpainted metal sheeting shall be used for roofing.

**Note:**
- (a) This exemption does not apply where a Special Amenity Area Order is in effect (see Appendix 2).
- (b) The structure can be located within 100m of the dwelling of the person providing it.

(c) It is advised that the County Council be consulted prior to erecting any structure as there is scope for disagreement due to the broad terms of this exemption. For example, "providing effluent storage appropriate to the size, location and use of the structure proposed" is open to interpretation.

### 3.4.2   Class 7 – Roofed Structures Housing Pigs, Mink or Poultry

The provision of a roofed structure as housing for:

- pigs;
- mink;
- poultry

does not require planning permission when all of the following are satisfied:

- The floor area does not exceed 75 sq. m (if the structure being provided is an extension, the limit for the original building and its extension is 75 sq. m combined).
- The structure is only used for agricultural purposes.
- The floor area of the building proposed does not exceed 100 sq. m when considered together with other such existing structures in the same farmyard complex OR any such buildings within 100m of the complex where the building is to be located.
- Effluent storage shall be provided that is appropriate to the size, use and location of the structure proposed in line with the requirements of the Department of Agriculture, Food and Rural Development and the Department of the Environment and Local Government .
- Water pollution by effluent shall be avoided.
- Effluent from the structure shall not be stored within 10m of a public road.
- The building proposed cannot be located within 10m of any public road.
- If the proposed building is located within 100m of the public road, its height cannot exceed 8m.
- The proposed building, or location for stored effluent from the building, shall not be located within 100m of a dwelling or "residential building", school, hospital, church or any building used for public "assembly" without the consent of the owner/occupier/person in charge of that property.
- No unpainted metal sheeting shall be used for roofing.
- A mink holding must have escape-proof boundary fencing.

**Note:**

This exemption does not apply where a Special Amenity Area Order is in effect (see Appendix 2).

### 3.4.3 Class 8 – Miscellaneous Farming Structures

The provision of:

- roofless cubicles;
- open loose yards;
- self-feed silo or silage areas;
- feeding aprons;
- assembly yards;
- milking parlours;
- structures for the making or storing of silage; or
- any other structures of a similar character with any ancillary effluent storage facility

does not require planning permission when all of the following are satisfied:

- The total site area of any proposed structure, when taken together with similar structures located in the same farmyard complex, does not exceed 200 sq. m. For example, it is proposed to construct an 80 sq. m milking parlour in a farmyard complex where there is an existing 150 sq. m milking parlour. This gives a total combined area for milking parlours of 230 sq. m. As this exceeds the 200 sq. m limit, planning permission would be required.
- The structure is only used for agriculture.
- The floor area of the development proposed does not exceed 300 sq. m when considered together with existing structures in the same farmyard complex OR any similar development within 100m of the complex where the building is to be located.
- Effluent storage shall be provided that is appropriate to the size, use and location of the structure proposed in line with the requirements of the Department of Agriculture, Food and Rural Development and the Department of the Environment and Local Government .
- Water pollution by effluent shall be avoided.
- Effluent from the structure shall not be stored within 10m of a public road.
- The structure proposed cannot be located within 10m of any public road.
- If the proposed structure is located within 100m of the public road, its height cannot exceed 8m.
- No unpainted metal sheeting shall be used for roofing.
- The proposed building, or location for stored effluent from the building, shall not be located within 100m of a dwelling or "residential building", school, hospital, church or any building used for public "assembly" without the consent of the owner/occupier/person in charge of that property.

**Note:**

(a) This exemption does not apply where a Special Amenity Area Order is in effect (see Appendix 2).

(b) The structure can be located within 100m of the dwelling of the person providing it.

(c) It is advised that the County Council be consulted prior to erecting any structure as there is scope for disagreement due to the broad terms of this exemption. For example, "providing effluent storage appropriate to the size, location and use of the structure proposed" is open to interpretation.

### 3.4.4    Class 9 – Stores, Barns, Glasshouses or Other Similar Structures

Class 9 exemptions relate to structures that are not covered by Classes 7 and 8 of this chapter. To be exempt from planning permission, the structure proposed must be a:

- barn;
- store;
- glasshouse; or
- "other structure" not described in Classes 7 and 8.

Furthermore, to be exempt from planning permission, the following conditions must be satisfied:

- The floor area of the structure does not exceed 300 sq. m.
- The structure is only used for agriculture or forestry.
- The structure is not used for storing effluent.
- The structure is not used for housing animals.
- The proposed floor area does not exceed 900 sq. m when considered together with "other such structures" in the same farmyard complex OR any similar structures within 100m of the complex where the proposed building is to be located.
- The structure cannot be located within 10m of any public road.
- If located within 100m of the public road, its height cannot exceed 8m.
- No unpainted metal sheeting shall be used for roofing.
- The proposed building, or location for stored effluent from the building, shall not be located within 100m of a dwelling or "residential building", school, hospital, church or any building used for public "assembly", without the consent of the owner/occupier/person in charge of that property.

**Note:**
(a) This exemption does not apply where a Special Amenity Area Order is in effect (see Appendix 2).
(b) The structure can be located within 100m of the dwelling of the person providing it.

### 3.4.5    Class 10 – Areas for Horses and Ponies

An unroofed fenced area can be provided for horses and ponies providing it is for exercise or training. Such a facility can have a drainage bed or soft surface material to provide for an all weather surface.

The facility:

- can only be used for the exercise of horses and ponies;
- must not be used for public events;
- cannot be located closer than 10m to a public road;
- cannot be accessed directly from a public road;
- shall not by higher than 2m.

**Note:**

This exemption does not apply where a Special Amenity Area Order is in effect (see Appendix 2).

### 3.4.6    Class 11 – Land Reclamation

As planning permission is ordinarily required for works carried out "on, in or under land", reclamation would normally require planning permission. However, certain works do not require planning permission when carried out on land ONLY used for agriculture and forestry. For example:

- draining fields;
- reclaiming land;
- removing fences;
- improving existing fences;
- improving hill grazing; or
- reclaiming callows or estuarine (river) marshes (the preservation of those marshes must not be an objective of the Development Plan for the area).

**Note:**

This exemption does not apply where a Special Amenity Area Order is in effect (see Appendix 2).

### 3.4.7    Class 12 – Kennels for Greyhounds

The provision of kennels for greyhounds does not require planning permission where all of the following conditions are satisfied:

- These kennels are only used for keeping greyhounds.
- Their floor area does not exceed 50 sq. m (if the structure being provided is an extension, the limit for the original building and its extension is 50 sq. m combined).
- The floor area of the building proposed does not exceed 75 sq. m when considered together with similar existing structures (for the same use) within the premises OR any buildings within 100m of the premises where the proposed kennels are to be built.
- Ancillary effluent storage shall be provided that is appropriate to the size, use and location of the structure proposed.

- Water pollution by effluent shall be avoided.
- Effluent from the structure shall not be stored within 10m of any public road.
- The building proposed cannot be located within 10m of any public road.
- If the proposed building is located within 100m of the public road, its height cannot exceed 8m.
- The proposed building, or location for stored effluent from the building, shall not be located within 100m of a dwelling or "residential building", school, hospital, church or any building used for public "assembly" without the consent of the owner/occupier/person in charge of that property.

**Note:**

(a) This exemption does not apply where a Special Amenity Area Order is in effect (See Appendix 2).

(b) The structure can be located within 100m of the dwelling of the person providing it.

(c) It is advised that the County Council be consulted prior to erecting any structure as there is scope for disagreement due to the broad terms of this exemption. For example, "providing effluent storage appropriate to the size, location and use of the structure proposed" is open to interpretation. Likewise, the interpretation of a building for "public assembly" and "residential building" may cause difficulties.

## 3.4.8    Class 13 – Provision of Hard Surface Areas for Use by Greyhounds

The provision of hard surface areas does not require planning permission when all of the following are satisfied:

- The hard surface area is roofless.
- The floor area does not exceed 100 sq. m (if the structure being provided is an extension, the limit for the original building and its extension is 100 sq. m combined).
- The development is used only in connection with the keeping of horses, ponies or greyhounds.
- The floor area of the development proposed does not exceed 150 sq. m when considered together with similar existing structures within the complex where its being located OR any similar such structures within 100m of the premises where the proposed development is to be.
- Effluent storage shall be provided that is appropriate to the size, use and location of the structure proposed.
- Water pollution by effluent shall be avoided.
- Effluent from the structure shall not be stored within 10m of any public road.
- The building proposed cannot be located within 10m of any public road.
- The proposed building, or location for stored effluent from the building, shall not be located within 100m of a dwelling or "residential building", school, hospital, church or any building used for public "assembly" without the consent of the owner/occupier/person in charge of that property.

**Note:**

(a) This exemption does not apply where a Special Amenity Area Order is in effect (see Appendix 2).

(b) The structure can be located within 100m of the dwelling of the person providing it.

(c) It is advised that the County Council be consulted prior to erecting any structure as there is scope for disagreement due to the broad terms of this exemption. For example, providing effluent storage "appropriate to the size, location and use of the structure proposed" is open to interpretation. Likewise, the interpretation of a building for "public assembly" and "residential building" may cause difficulties.

### 3.4.9    Class 14 – Intensive Agriculture

The use of uncultivated land or semi-natural land for intensive agricultural purposes is exempt from planning permission where the area is less than 100 hectares.

### 3.4.10    Class 15 – Afforestation

Initial afforestation of land is exempt. However, an EIS (Environmental Impact Statement) is required for initial afforestation of 50 Ha. or more and this development is not exempt.

### 3.4.11    Class 16 – Afforestation (Broadleaf)

The replacement of broadleaf high forest by conifer species is exempt where the area involved is less than 10 Ha. Any area greater than that will require an EIS.

### 3.4.12    Class 17 – Peat Extraction

Peat extraction in a new area or an extended area of less than 10 Ha. is exempt from the requirement to obtain planning permission. Similarly, peat extraction in a new area or an extended area of more than 10 Ha. where the drainage of the lands commenced prior to these Regulations coming into force (March 2002), is exempt from planning permission.

# Appendix 1

## Section 5 References

Under section 5 of the Planning and Development Act 2000 it is possible to make an official submission to the Planning Authority (Local Authority) in which the development is proposed in order to ascertain their view as to whether it requires planning permission or not. This procedure is particularly useful where there may be some doubt over whether or not a development is exempted development due to its location or otherwise. There is a fee for making such a submission and at the time of writing (mid 2002) this fee is €80. In order for the Planning Authority to make determination, sufficient information must be provided. Generally this would involve drawings and details of the development proposed, including its location and character.

Should you disagree with the views of the Planning Authority, you may then appeal the decision to An Bord Pleanála.

More information on the procedure to be followed is available from your local Planning Office.

# Appendix 2A

## Restrictions on Exemptions – General

Article 9 of the Planning Regulations identifies a number of instances where exemptions do not apply, *i.e.* planning permission will be required no matter how minor the development. In summary, development is "de-exempted" in the general circumstances outlined below. The text of Article 9 of the Planning Regulations is included at the end of this Appendix.

**Breaking the conditions of a planning permission:** If you wish to place an extension on a house, the design of which complies with the conditions contained in the Regulations, planning permission is still required if a condition has been attached to a previous planning permission for the house which stipulates that no extensions can be constructed without further permission.

**Being inconsistent with any use specified in a planning permission:** This effectively means, for example, that exemptions allowing for rural developments could not be applied where a property has been granted planning permission for residential purposes.

**Making or widening an access to a surfaced public road exceeding 4m in width:** Where the work proposed involves the making, laying out, or material widening of an access (*e.g.* a gateway) to a surfaced public road where the surfaced carriageway of that road exceeds 4m in width, the relevant planning exemptions do not apply.

**Creating a danger to public safety through traffic hazard or obstruction of road users:** This is a very flexible restriction on the applicability of exemptions.

**Breaking a building line:** This will also render the exemption inapplicable, unless the development is a porch consistent with Class 7 of Chapter 1. This also applies if the "building line" is specified in a Development Plan or a Draft Development Plan.

**Development under a public road:** Development of anything other than connections to services such as sewers, gas, water and "wired broadcast relay services" (*e.g.* Eircom) requires planning permission.

**"Interfering" with the "character of a landscape" or a view or prospect:** Blocking a view that is listed in either the Development Plan or any Draft Development Plan for the area in which development is proposed will render the exemption inapplicable. The restriction may cause some difficulties depending on the nature of the development proposed, *i.e.* to what extent does a small advertising sign "interfere" with a view or prospect. Most Planning Authorities are now preparing Landscape Character Assessments which will establish a further set of criteria by which proposed

83

exempted developments will have to be evaluated. It is advisable that if you have a significant (and visible) development located in a rural area, for example an initial afforestation of land less than 50 Ha., you should check with the Planning Authority initially to ensure that it is not contrary to their Landscape Character Assessment (if one has been prepared) or has not been de-exempted by its provisions.

**Altering a designated/listed site of natural, historical or archaeological importance:** *i.e.* sites listed in a Development Plan or a Draft Development Plan.

**Consolidating an unauthorised site or use:** Extending, altering, repairing or renewing a development or use that does not have planning permission in the first instance, means that no exemption can be applied.

**Altering a protected structure:** Carrying out of works to a protected structure, or a proposed protected structure, is exempt from the need to obtain planning permission only if those works would not materially affect the character of—

(a) the structure; or

(b) any element of the structure which contributes to its special architectural, historical, archaeological, artistic, cultural, scientific, social or technical interest.

It is very important to check any such proposals with a Planning Authority prior to developing them as to whether or not the character of a protected structure is altered, as this can in many cases be a subjective matter of opinion.

**Altering a building/property in an Architectural Conservation Area or a proposed Architectural Conservation Area:** The carrying out of works to the exterior of a structure located in an Architectural Conservation area or a proposed Architectural Conservation Area requires planning permission only if those works materially affect the character of the area.

It is very important to check any such proposals with a Planning Authority prior to developing them as to whether or not the character of an area is altered, as this can in many cases be a subjective matter of opinion.

**Precluding the Continuance of a Required Use:** If the demolition or alteration of an existing building or structure precludes the continuance of a use where that continuation is an objective of the Planning Authority (and that objective is specified in the Development Plan), then that alteration/demolition is not exempt.

**Restricting access to a location of public beauty/recreational utility that has been habitually open to or used by the public during the 10 years preceding such obstruction:** This has particular implications for developments in a rural area.

**Enclosing land which has been habitually open to the public in the preceding 10 years:** This will render an exemption inapplicable.

**Restricting/obstructing a right of way:** This will render an exemption inapplicable.

**Development being located in an area where a Special Amenity Area Order applies:** Planning permission will generally be required in this situation. This also applies where an industrial activity is involved or involves the storage of hazardous materials.

Where a Special Amenity Area Order applies, the following exemptions are specifically restricted:

Chapter 1: Class 1, 3, 11, 16, 21, 22, 27, 28, 29, 31 (except underground equipment), 33 (for athletics or sports where there is no charge to the public for admission and including the laying out and use of land for golf or pitch and putt or sports involving the use of motor vehicles, aircraft or firearms), 39, 44 or 50 (the demolition of a building or a structure).

Chapter 2: The use of a structure or other land for the exhibition of advertisements of Class 1, 4, 6, 11, 16 or 17.

Chapter 3: Class 3, 5, 6, 7, 8, 9, 10, 11, 12 or 13.

You should note that where development is necessary in order to give effect to a condition attached to an IPC licence (either new or revised) granted by the Environmental Protection Agency under Part IV of the said Act, this shall be exempted development. (See section 84(4)(a) of the Environmental Protection Agency Act 1992 and Local Government (Planning and Development) Regulations 1995, Statutory Instrument No. 69 of 1995.)

**Note:**
  (a) Any development that requires an Environmental Impact Statement also cannot be exempt from planning permission unless it is permitted under another Act or in order to comply with an EU Directive.
  (b) Exempted development that may give rise to a modification of a development so that it may have significant repercussions on Major Accident Hazards is also similarly de-exempted.
  (c) Where an Order under section 202 of the Planning and Development Act 2002 is in place limiting exempted development rights, exemptions are limited as per the terms of the Order.
  (d) The full text of the Article 9 restrictions on exemptions as contained in the Planning Regulations is given in the following Appendix 2B.

# Appendix 2B

## Article 9 – Restrictions on Exemption (as contained in the Planning Regulations 2001)

Article 9(1) Development to which article 6 relates shall not be exempted development for the purposes of the Act –

(a) if the carrying out of such development would:

  (i) contravene a condition attached to a permission under the Act or be inconsistent with any use specified in a permission under the Act;

  (ii) consist of or comprise the formation, laying out or material widening of a means of access to a public road the surfaced carriageway of which exceeds 4m in width;

  (iii) endanger public safety by reason of traffic hazard or obstruction of road users;

  (iv) except in the case of a porch to which Class 7 specified in column 1 of Part 1 of Schedule 2 applies, and which complies with the conditions and limitations specified in column 2 of the said Part 1 opposite the mention of that class in the said column 1, comprise the construction, erection, extension or renewal of a building on any street so as to bring forward the building, or any part of the building, beyond the front wall of the building on either side thereof or beyond a line determined as the building line in a development plan for the area or, pending the variation of a development plan or the making of a new development plan, in the draft variation of the development plan or the draft development plan;

  (v) consist of or comprise the carrying out under a public road of works other than a connection to a wired broadcast relay service, sewer, water main, gas main or electricity supply line or cable, or any works to which Class 25, 26 or 31(a) specified in column 1 of Part 1 of Schedule 2 applies;

  (vi) interfere with the character of a landscape, or a view or prospect of special amenity value or special interest, the preservation of which is an objective of a development plan for the area in which the development is proposed or, pending the variation of a development plan or the making of a new development plan, in the draft variation of the development plan or the draft development plan;

  (vii) consist of or comprise the excavation, alteration or demolition (other than peat extraction) of places, caves, sites, features or other objects of archaeological, geological, historical, scientific or ecological interest, the preservation of which is an objective of a development plan for the area in which the development is proposed or, pending the variation of a development plan or the making of a new development plan, in the draft variation of the development plan or the draft development plan, save any excavation, pursuant to and in accordance with a licence granted under section 26 of the National Monuments Act 1930 (No. 2 of 1930);

(viii) consist of or comprise the extension, alteration, repair or renewal of an unauthorised structure or a structure the use of which is unauthorised;

(ix) consist of the demolition or such alteration of a building or other structure as would preclude or restrict the continuance of an existing use of a building or other structure where it is an objective of the planning authority to ensure that the building or other structure would remain available for such use and such objective has been specified in a development plan for the area or, pending the variation of a development plan or the making of a new development plan, in the draft variation of the development plan or the draft development plan;

(x) consist of the fencing or enclosure of any land habitually open to or used by the public during the 10 years preceding such fencing or enclosure for recreational purposes or as a means of access to any seashore, mountain, lakeshore, riverbank or other place of natural beauty or recreational utility,

(xi) obstruct any public right of way;

(xii) further to the provisions of section 82 of the Act, consist of or comprise the carrying out of works to the exterior of a structure, where the structure concerned is located within an architectural conservation area or an area specified as an architectural conservation area in a development plan for the area or, pending the variation of a development plan or the making of a new development plan, in the draft variation of the development plan or the draft development plan and the development would materially affect the character of the area.

(b) in an area to which a special amenity area order relates, if such development would be development:

(i) of Class 1, 3, 11, 16, 21, 22, 27, 28, 29, 31 (other than paragraph (a) thereof ), 33(c) (including the laying out and use of land for golf or pitch and putt or sports involving the use of motor vehicles, aircraft or firearms), 39, 44 or 50(a) specified in column 1 of Part 1 of Schedule 2; or

(ii) consisting of the use of a structure or other land for the exhibition of advertisements of Class 1, 4, 6, 11, 16 or 17 specified in column 1 of Part 2 of the said Schedule or the erection of an advertisement structure for the exhibition of any advertisement of any of the said classes; or

(iii) of Class 3, 5, 6, 7, 8, 9, 10, 11, 12 or 13 specified in column 1 of Part 3 of the said Schedule; or

(iv) of any class of Parts 1, 2 or 3 of Schedule 2 not referred to in sub-paragraphs (i), (ii) and (iii) where it is stated in the Order made under section 202 of the Act that such development shall be prevented or limited.

(c) if it is development to which Part 10 applies, unless the development is required by or under any statutory provision (other than the Act or these Regulations) to comply with procedures for the purpose of giving effect to the Council Directive;

(d) if it consists of the provision of, or modifications to, an establishment, and could have significant repercussions on major accident hazards.

Sub-article (1)(a)(vi) shall not apply where the development consists of the construction by any electricity undertaking of an overhead line or cable not exceeding 100m in length for the purpose of conducting electricity from a distribution or transmission line to any premises.

# Appendix 3

## Important Definitions

The following are the specific definitions used in the Planning Regulations for particular types of use such as shops and amusement arcades. They are very important when considering changes of use and should always be examined prior to advising as to whether a development does or does not require planning permission.

## Exempted Development

"aerodrome" means any definite and limited area (including water) intended to be used, either wholly or in part, for or in connection with the landing or departure of aircraft.

"airport" means an area of land comprising an aerodrome and any buildings, roads and car parks connected to the aerodrome and used by the airport authority in connection with the operation thereof.

"airport operational building" means a building other than a hotel, required in connection with the movement or maintenance of aircraft, or with the embarking, disembarking, loading, discharge or transport of passengers, livestock or goods at an airport.

"amusement arcade" means premises used for the playing of gaming machines, video games or other amusement games.

"betting office" means premises for the time being registered in the register of bookmaking offices kept by the Revenue Commissioners under the Betting Act 1931 (No. 27 of 1931).

"business premises" means —

(a) any structure or other land (not being an excluded premises) which is normally used for the carrying on of any professional, commercial or industrial undertaking or any structure (not being an excluded premises) which is normally used for the provision therein of services to persons;

(b) a hotel or public house;

(c) any structure or other land used for the purposes of, or in connection with, the functions of a State authority.

"care" means personal care, including help with physical or social needs.

"childminding" means the activity of minding no more than six children, including the children, if any, of the person minding, in the house of that person, for profit or gain;

"day centre" means non-residential premises used for social or recreational purposes or for the provision of care (including occupational training).

"Director of Telecommunications Regulation" means the Director of Telecommunications Regulation appointed under the Telecommunications (Miscellaneous Provisions) Act 1996 (No. 34 of 1996);

"excluded premises" means—

(a) any premises used for purposes of a religious, educational, cultural, recreational or medical character;

(b) any guest house or other premises (not being a hotel) providing overnight guest accommodation, block of flats or apartments, club, boarding house or hostel;

(c) any structure which was designed for use as one or more separate dwellings, except such a structure which was used as business premises immediately before October 1, 1964 or is so used with permission under the Act.

"fish counter" means a device capable of mechanically or electrically enumerating fish as they pass a specific point or area.

"Greater Dublin Area" means the area comprising the County Borough of Dublin and the administrative counties of Dun Laoghaire-Rathdown, Fingal, Kildare, Meath, South Dublin and Wicklow.

"house" does not, as regards development of Class 1, 2, 3, 4, 6(b)(ii), 7 or 8 specified in column 1 of Part 1 of Schedule 2, or development to which Articles 10(4) or 10(5) refer, include a building designed for use or used as two or more dwellings or a flat, an apartment or other dwelling within such a building.

"illuminated" in relation to any advertisement, sign or other advertisement structure means illuminated internally or externally by artificial lighting, directly or by reflection, for the purpose of advertisement, announcement or direction.

"industrial building" means a structure (not being a shop, or a structure in or adjacent to and belonging to a quarry or mine) used for the carrying on of any industrial process.

"light industrial building" means an industrial building in which the processes carried on or the plant or machinery installed are such as could be carried on or installed in any residential area without detriment to the amenity of that area by reason of noise, vibration, smell, fumes, smoke, soot, ash, dust or grit.

"industrial process" means any process which is carried on in the course of trade or business other than agriculture and which is for or incidental to the making of any article or part of an article (including a vehicle, aircraft, ship or vessel, or a film, broadcast, cable programme, publication and computer programme and any original database, video or sound recording), or the altering, repairing, ornamenting, finishing, cleaning, washing, packing, canning, adapting for sale, breaking up or demolition of any article, including the getting, dressing or treatment of minerals.

"industrial undertaker" means a person by whom an industrial process is carried on and "industrial undertaking" shall be construed accordingly.

"mobile telephony"" means public mobile telephony.

"painting" includes any application of colour.

"repository" means a structure (excluding any land occupied therewith) where storage is the principal use and where no business is transacted other than business incidental to such storage.

"shop" means a structure used for any or all of the following purposes, where the sale, display or service is principally to visiting members of the public:

(a)  for the retail sale of goods;

(b)  as a post office;

(c)  for the sale of tickets or as a travel agency;

(d)  for the sale of sandwiches or other food for consumption off the premises where the sale of such food is subsidiary to the main retail use;

(e)  for hairdressing;

(f)  for the display of goods for sale;

(g)  for the hiring out of domestic or personal goods or articles;

(h)  as a launderette or dry cleaners;

(i)  for the reception of goods to be washed, cleaned or repaired

but does not include use for the provision of funeral services or as a funeral home, or as a hotel, a restaurant or a public house, or for the sale of hot food for consumption off the premises except under (d) above where it is ancillary to the main use of the shop, or any use to which class 2 or 3 of Part IV of the Second Schedule applies (see Chapter One, Class 14).

"supermarket" means a self-service shop selling mainly food.

"telecommunications network" means the whole of the telecommunications infrastructure and any associated physical infrastructure of any network operator.

"telecommunications service" means services which consist wholly or partly of the transmission or routing of signals on a telecommunications network or both transmission and routing.

"wholesale warehouse" means a structure where business, principally of a wholesale nature, is transacted and goods are stored or displayed but only incidentally to the transaction of that business.

"height" – unless the context otherwise requires, any reference to the height of a structure, plant or machinery shall be construed as a reference to its height when measured from ground level, and for that purpose "ground level" means the level of the ground immediately adjacent to the structure, plant or machinery or, where the level of the ground where it is situated or is to be situated is not uniform, the level of the lowest part of the ground adjacent to it.

"curtilage" – the Planning Acts and Regulations use the word "curtilage" to essentially describe the grounds of a property on which a use takes place. This may be subject to debate, however, as the term is flexible in its interpretation in cases.

# Index

## (references are to paragraph numbers)